WORKPLACE EQUALITY IN EUROPE

Workplace Equality in Europe

The Role of Trade Unions

ANNA PARASKEVOPOULOU AND SONIA MCKAY
both at London Metropolitan University, UK

ASHGATE

Published by
Ashgate Publishing Limited
Wey Court East
Union Road
Farnham
Surrey, GU9 7PT
England

Ashgate Publishing Company
110 Cherry Street
Suite 3-1
Burlington, VT 05401-3818
USA

www.ashgate.com

British Library Cataloguing in Publication Data
A catalogue record for this book is available from the British Library.

The Library of Congress has cataloged the printed edition as follows:
Paraskevopoulou, Anna.
Workplace equality in Europe : the role of trade unions / by Anna Paraskevopoulou and Sonia McKay.
   pages cm
Includes bibliographical references and index.
ISBN 978-1-4724-2671-0 (hardback) – ISBN 978-1-4724-2672-7 (ebook) –
ISBN 978-1-4724-2673-4 (epub) 1. Discrimination in employment–European Union countries. 2. Diversity in the workplace–European Union countries. 3. Labor unions– European Union countries. I. McKay, Sonia. II. Title.
HD4903.5.E85P368 2015
331.13'3094–dc23

                                                                          2014037672

ISBN: 9781472426710 (hbk)
ISBN: 9781472426727 (ebk – PDF)
ISBN: 9781472426734 (ebk – ePUB)

Printed in the United Kingdom by Henry Ling Limited, at the Dorset Press, Dorchester, DT1 1HD

Contents

Acknowledgements

This book would not have been possible without the invaluable help of our colleagues at the Working Lives Research Institute, London Metropolitan University. In particular we would like to thank Eugenia Markova, Janroj Keles, Leena Kumarappan, Jawad Botmeh, Janet Emefo and Max Watson. Last but not least we would like to thank Richard Meheux for his input in the final editing of the book.

As the book has drawn on aspects of the Mapping research we would of course extend our thanks to all those who participated in that project.

The authors alone take responsibility for any errors in this book.

List of Abbreviations

3F	United Federation of Danish Workers
ASI	Icelandic Confederation of Labour
CCOO	Trade Union Confederation of Workers' Commissions, Spain
CGIL	Italian General Confederation of Labour
CGT	General Confederation of Labour, France
CGTP	General Confederation of Portuguese Workers
CITUB	Confederation of Independent Trade Unions, Bulgaria
CNS Cartel Alfa	National Confederation of Trade Unions, Romania
CNV	National Federation of Christian Trade Unions, Netherlands
CNV Jongeren	Christian Youth Trade Union, Netherlands
CNVO	CNV Education, Netherlands
CSC	Confederation of Christian Trade Unions, Belgium
CSIL	Italian Confederation of Workers' Trade Unions
CWU	UK Communications Workers Union
DELTA	Public Sector Union, Norway
DEOK	The Democratic Labour Federation of Cyprus
EDF	European Disability Forum
EHRC	Equality and Human Rights Commission, UK
EIRO	European Industrial Relations Observatory
EKA	Athens Labour Centre, Greece
ENAR	European Network Against Racism
ETUC	European Trade Union Confederation
ETUCE	European Trade Union Committee for Education
ETUI	European Trade Union Institute
Eurofound	European Foundation for the Improvement of Living and Working Conditions
EWCs	European Works Councils
FBU	Fire Brigades Union, UK
FGTB	General Federation of Belgian Labour
FNV	Netherlands Trade Union Confederation
FNV Jong	Netherlands Trade Union Federation Young
FOA	Danish Union of Public Employees
FRA	European Union Agency for Fundamental Rights
GMB	Britain's General Union

Handels	Commercial Workers Union, Sweden
IG BAU	The German Trade Union for
	Building, Forestry, Agriculture and the Environment
ILGA – Europe	European Region of the International
	Lesbian, Gay, Bisexual, Trans and Intersex Association
IMPACT	Irish Municipal, Public and Civil Trade Union
INTO	Irish National Teachers' Organisation
ITUC	International Trade Union Confederation
KOZ SR	Slovakian Confederation of Trade Unions
LIGA	Democratic Confederation
	of Free Trade Unions, Hungary
NSZZ	Independent and Self-
	Governing Trade Union Solidarnosc, Poland
OAJ	Trade Union of Education, Finland
OEGB	Austrian Federation of Trade Unions
OEGB OO	Regional organisation of
	the Austrian Federation of Trade Unions
OEGJ	Youth organisation of the
	Austrian Federation of Trade Unions
OGBL	Trade Union Confederation, Luxembourg
OLME	Federation of Secondary School Teachers, Greece
OPZZ	All Poland Alliance of Trade Unions
Petricontex	Federation of Light Industry Trade Unions, Romania
Podkrepa	Bulgarian Confederation of Labour
TIB	Timber, Industry and
	Construction Workers' Union, Denmark
TUC	Trades Union Congress, UK
UEN	Union of Education Norway
UGT	General Workers' Union, Spain
UHM	United Workers' Union, Malta
UIL	Italian Union of Labour
UIL Scuola	Uil's Federation of Education Workers, Italy
UNISON	Public Service Trade Union, UK
USOC	Workers' Union, Spain
Verdi	German public sector union Verdi
ZNP	Polish Teacher Union
ZSSS	Association of Free Trade Unions of Slovenia
ZZPE	Polish Electric Machine Industry Union

Chapter 1
Introduction

Despite a long European labour history of fighting inequalities in the workplace and in society as a whole, through the development of social movements, trade unions, political parties and pressure groups, discrimination persists and permeates most aspects of our contemporary lives. In terms of employment, discrimination can be present in the process of recruitment, career promotion and development, income and benefits, opportunities for training and in day-to-day workplace contact. Although definitions and types of discrimination may vary according to different social trends, conscience and understandings, it can be argued that discrimination itself occurs directly when one person is treated less favourably than another because of certain characteristics.

Since 2000, the European Union has adopted several new measures on combating discrimination based on sex, race and ethnicity, disability, religion and belief, sexual orientation and age for younger or older people. These measures include equality directives, the funding of national policies and measures for the promotion of equality, the dissemination of good practice and the funding of projects designed to tackle discrimination in the workplace through the funding streams of EQUAL and the European Social Fund. Two key developments, explored in this book, are the anti-discrimination directives: Council Directive (2000/78/EC), on establishing a general framework for equal treatment in employment and occupation, and Council Directive (2000/43/EC), on implementing the principle of equal treatment between persons irrespective of racial or ethnic origin which provide protection based on the five separate strands of discrimination. Furthermore, the Charter of Fundamental Rights of 2000 reaffirms the principle of non-discrimination as one of the commitments of the European Union adding seven additional grounds: social origin, genetic features, language, political or other opinion, membership of a national minority and property and birth.[1]

At the same time, especially since 2000, and as a result of European policies encouraging a neoliberal economic system accompanied by neoliberal trends in employment, we have started to see the weakening of employment legislation across Europe and a surge in 'flexible' or atypical forms of work which do not

---

1 http://europa.eu/legislation_summaries/other/l14157_en.htm (accessed in June 2014).

provide the same security or welfare benefits as standard employment.[2] Research has shown that atypical forms of employment affect mainly groups of workers with one or more protected characteristic, such as women, migrant workers and older or younger people who experience a higher risk of unemployment, forced part-time employment, badly paid work, precarious work conditions, issues related to poor health and safety and ultimately the threat of living below the poverty line. The promotion of such policies should not be seen as separate from other EU policies especially as this is a period of deep economic crisis and one where rapid socioeconomic changes are taking place, such as the shrinking of public services and social security systems or the privatisation of social services, for example, education and health. Therefore, it can be argued that as a result of these neoliberal economic policies adopted by the EU and by Member States, there is a continuous threat of weakening and downgrading the work already been carried out in relation to equality and anti-discrimination legislation, and ultimately to the protection of European citizens. We detail a number of cases where initiatives have been developed nationally as well as through cross-border or international cooperation, to assist vulnerable workers, through union representation or awareness of employment rights.

Within this context, this book looks at the work of trade unions across Europe in supporting equality and anti-discrimination policies. Their role within the European Union is important as they participate in the process of European social dialogue but also seek to influence European policies. Dickens argues that trade unions are very effective in 'helping translate formal rights into substantial change at workplace' (2007: 484) and in developing good equality practice. Heery (2006), in his research on equality bargaining, found that in the UK, trade unions had been active in promoting gender equality while the issue of 'equal pay' was well incorporated in their bargaining agenda. As agents of equality, trade unions can have a dual role in its promotion: first, through their internal structures as employers and second, through their external actions in their negotiations with employers and their general campaigning (Greene and Kirton, 2004). The central argument of this book is that legislation alone does not combat discrimination; it is important to look at the social structures and processes that give rise to prejudices and discrimination in order to explore a general framework that might challenge social inequalities and understand the role of social actors in this effort. Throughout the book we ask questions about the actions and challenges faced by trade unions in implementing anti-discrimination policies at local, national and European levels. As a method of analysis the study of trade union initiatives is not assessed merely on their outcomes but also in terms of their impact for influencing trade union

---

2 See for example McKay, S. Jefferys, S. Paraskevopoulou, A. and Keles, J. (2012) *Study on precarious work and social rights*, European Commission.

behaviour especially at local and national levels – as discussed in subsequent chapters – and for providing the basis or the impetus for further action and for higher cooperation with unions in other Member States.

The book draws its data both from secondary and primary sources. Secondary sources include the use of documents or data from European based trade unions such as the European Trade Union Confederation (ETUC), the European Trade Union Institute (ETUI) and the European Trade Union Committee for Education (ETUCE); from European based NGOs such as ILGA-Europe, AGE Platform Europe, the European Disability Forum and the European Network Against Racism (ENAR); data from the Organisation for Economic Co-operation and Development (OECD) and data from Eurobarometer; documents and previous studies from European organisations such as the European Commission, the European Foundation for the Improvement of Living and Working Conditions (Eurofound), the European Union Agency for Fundamental Rights (FRA); as well as other academic resources. The book also uses some of the data and case studies of selective initiatives from the Mapping study which was carried by Working Lives Research Institute between 2009 and 2010 and gathered information of the initiatives of trade unions and Non-Governmental Organisations (NGOs) developed to tackle discrimination and promote equality and diversity in the workplace. The research involved 27 Member States, the EFTA/EEA States (Iceland, Liechtenstein and Norway) and three then candidate countries (Croatia,[3] Turkey and the Former Yugoslav Republic of Macedonia) and one potential then candidate, Serbia.[4] The main methods used for the Mapping study included literature reviews, over 250 in-depth face-to-face interviews with trade union senior representatives in 34 European states, as well as with representatives of around 70 NGOs, exploring their views, perceptions and understandings of the two European directives and on the basis of these developed 15 case studies of initiatives. The main focus of the Mapping research was on five out of six grounds of discrimination: racial and ethnic origin, religion and belief, age, disability and sexual orientation. The Mapping study did not cover the strand of gender but it did try to understand if gender had been mainstreamed in anti-discrimination actions by trade unions. An overall finding suggests that whilst gender was discussed in the interviews, only a small minority of trade unions mainstreamed gender when developing anti-discrimination programmes or initiatives.

---

3 Since 2013 Croatia became an EU Member state.

4 For more information on Serbia see http://ec.europa.eu/enlargement/countries/detailed-country-information/serbia/index_en.htm (accessed July 2014).

Outline

The book draws on some of the main themes identified and explored in the Mapping study and consists of nine chapters. Chapter 2 provides the theoretical context, explaining the relationship between equality and diversity, equal opportunities and the business case for diversity. We argue, first, that inequalities are socially constructed and deep rooted in most aspects of our social life. At work inequalities lead to segregations, with groups who face negative stereotyping often holding lower positions and having inferior work conditions. Second, we argue that although legislation and policy interventions are vital in addressing matters of discrimination, these alone are not adequate to tackle the socially embedded prejudices and attitudes that contribute to the direct or indirect acts and polices of discrimination. The chapter also considers alternative approaches on individual and group differences and on different models represented in the workplace to address disadvantages and discrimination. The second part of the chapter focuses on the role of trade unions and sets the context to understand the way the concepts of *equality* and *diversity* came to influence public policy and practice in Europe. We make the argument here that despite declining membership, trade unions are still large organisations and are considered key social actors in European social dialogue. In addition both European Directives (Council Directive (2000/43/EC) and Council Directive (2000/78/EC) impose specific obligations on trade unions to promote equal treatment in their negotiations and social dialogue, collective agreements, policies, research and good practice.

Chapter 3 looks at disadvantage and discrimination in the labour market within a wider context. Negative stereotyping, prejudices and the exclusion of particular groups are explored by examining the role of European legislation and more specifically the two key European Directives in providing protection for the different strands of discrimination. Citing Zick et al. (2008) and Ahmet et al. (2013), the chapter argues that prejudice and discrimination, both of which feed into stereotypes, are a widespread phenomenon in Europe, even in Member States that are most commonly viewed as tolerant, such as for example Sweden where a recent study found that discrimination on the basis of sexual orientation was still evident. Key findings are examined in the chapter, through a detailed critique of the legislative approach itself and there is discussion on questions such as how can the law affect changes in the workplace and how can the law influence the behaviour of key workplace actors. The chapter also looks at the role of trade unions as social dialogue partners and with a key responsibility for the effective implementation of equality and non-discrimination, limited only by those regulatory measures established under national law or practice. It is without question that the trade unions should be well-placed to promote equality since they will have direct knowledge of cases or potential cases of discrimination. The chapter concludes that trade union involvement is vital, beyond just providing information on the content of the Directives to providing support for the victims of discrimination. But at the same time there are also challenges which can undermine trade union involvement, as there are questions on competence in dealing with the complexities of anti-discrimination legislation which are often combined with the high costs of taking claims and the high risks of failure, as it is often the case in discrimination cases. In its final section the chapter argues that policies to ensure equality of treatment have been challenged in a period of economic crisis, as governments, employers and other social actors have promoted measures that weaken employment laws and have a potential to undermine equality.

Chapter 4 is the first of the chapters in this book that focuses more specifically on trade union work on anti-discrimination and sets the context for the thematic exploration of initiatives in chapters that follow. The chapter examines trade union practices at European level which were identified in the Mapping study, particularly those that involved trade union engagement with NGOs. Here we overview policies reported to the Mapping study by the European level trade unions and explore what has happened to these initiatives since the time when they were first developed. This overview does not cover every policy adopted by European level trade unions but only those reported to the Mapping study and which the study had identified as significant or innovative by the trade unions themselves. The chapter tries to understand the nature of these initiatives in more detail by looking at their type, duration and longer-term impact and asks questions such as why certain initiatives were pursued; what the context was for their development and implementation; and why some initiatives appeared to have greater resonance or have a more long-lasting impact than others. The chapter concludes that these European wide initiatives helped to bring trade unions and NGOs closer together in their work on anti-discrimination, each benefiting from understanding different working structures and practices. However a challenge to these initiatives was that most were dependent on external funding, mainly from the European Union, and as a result they were often not sustainable once funding had ended. Another challenge was that the main theme or action of the initiatives was selected or determined by the requirements of the funders.

One emerging theme from the Mapping study was that some trade union activities were based on cross country cooperation, due in part to higher worker mobility in the last decade but also because companies have spread out from the national borders, as recent research has identified, for example Gold and Rees (2013), Pulignano (2005) and Waddington and Hoffmann (2000). Chapter 5 looks at relevant findings and argues that while formal structures, such as European Works Councils (EWCs), enabled cooperation between trade unions in different European states, cooperation also takes place when formal structures have not been set up and therefore it is important to look at the enabling mechanisms that foster trans-national activities. This is especially important in a period of economic instability which often leads to the breaking up of existing structures. The chapter identifies seven drivers that encourage transnational cooperation and they are: Member States sharing common borders; pre-existing EWCs have operated as models of engagement; existing trans-national cooperation between labour sending and labour receiving states; existing involvement of EU level institutions; access to EU level funds; trade union policies specifically in relation to working with developing countries; and collaboration between trade unions and NGOs. Using Larsson's concepts of 'hard' and 'soft' issues, the chapter shows how transnational cooperation has not only brought tangible results but also allowed trade unions to challenge some of their own stereotypes or those held by their members. And cooperation with EU level organisations has opened up options for national trade unions to explore other routes for working against discrimination at work and in society as a whole.

As well as cooperation between trade unions and NGOs at European level, the Mapping research found that links between trade unions and NGOs also existed at national level. Chapter 6 explores these relationships in their work against discrimination and discusses the benefits and challenges of their coexistence. Existing literature shows that this relationship was uneasy at its beginning; however in recent years closer ties have developed between the two, as both are civil organisations with main agendas and strategies in improving the living conditions of people and workers and such collaborations can contribute to more effective ways of fighting for equality (Gallin, 2000) while making a dynamic contribution to civil society and the democratic process on both European and international levels. The Mapping study found three main factors for the development of such collaborations. First, the influence of the European Union through its work with the European level trade unions on the one hand and with the European level NGOs on the other, or as a result of EU funding for major projects which encourage partnerships and social dialogue. Second, closer ties are the result of migration movements which have increased as globalisation advanced and which led to unions seeking closer links with countries outside Europe in order to either carry out work in these countries or to develop better links with unions in these countries. Work with NGOs in this respect was beneficial as it provided easier access to the new countries. Finally, the Mapping research found some evidence of trade unions helping to set up NGOs, which functioned independently but helped carry out collaborative work in developing countries. Similar methods were used for cooperation at international level.

Chapter 7 focuses on the concept of multiple discrimination. Although the Mapping study did not specifically set out to gather information in this area, it assumed that discrimination is widespread in European societies and therefore it sought to understand certain complexities of inequality itself, to identify any interrelations between the different strands of discrimination and to explore the type of equality and diversity provisions supported by the trade unions. It is argued that multiple discrimination had been partly conceptualised and reflected on in the planning of trade union equality initiatives, since they had focused on tackling inequalities at all levels of society. The first part of the chapter looks at the development of the concept within a historical context located within the academic socio-legal debates of the black feminist movement, mainly in the US. The second part concentrates on the development of relevant policies, more specifically in relation to trade unions. The research found that overall there has been limited engagement with the concept of multiple discrimination by trade unions in Europe. In some cases trade unions adopted more traditional ways to fight discrimination as a whole rather than on separate strands; in other cases there was a limited understanding of the concept itself; in some cases the weakness of the legal systems to adopt measures for protecting the victims of multiple discrimination was reflected in trade union policies; and finally there were cases where multiple discrimination was conceptualised through a more generic gender mainstreaming approach adopted by the trade unions which in practical terms it meant that some strands of discrimination had been combined with gender, such as for example gender and age, or gender and disability. The chapter concludes that more awareness is needed in the area of multiple discrimination and more effort is required from policy makers as well as trade unions. In legal terms there is a need for a legal structure to provide protection for the victims.

Chapter 8 looks at the impact of the economic crisis on implementing equality policies, as research has shown that even at the start of the crisis income, disparities between the rich and poor had grown, leading to a rise in social inequality and poverty within European Member States. The topic of economic crisis was not directly addressed by the Mapping study, however the research itself took place at the start of the economic downturn and inevitably respondents discussed their views. A main concern voiced was the threat of a potential rise of racial tensions against migrants and ethnic minorities who were viewed as competitors in a shrinking labour market. Research participants also discussed the increased risk of precarious work conditions for migrant workers, especially those with undocumented status, as well as other 'vulnerable' groups. During the time of the Mapping study, strong anti-immigration agendas were already being discussed and implemented in Member States, as well as criticisms being articulated about the role and function of the European Union itself. The chapter argues that under this climate it becomes more challenging for trade unions to develop equality policies, although some had found the tools to continue and pursue their equality aims, but for others this was not the case. It was suggested that unions with weak commitments to equality in general were more likely to cite the economic crisis as a reason for inactivity and those with stronger commitments to equality more likely to try and secure their equality initiatives or policies.

With Chapter 9, the book concludes with a reflection on the wider role of trade unions in promoting equality in the workplace, even under the challenges of the economic crisis, their partnerships and their working practices for the future. Fanelli and Brogan (2014) argue for a bottom up approach in organising and in building community labour coalitions, as well as for a need for unions to reinvent themselves as a way of fighting austerity more effectively. The chapter suggests that many trade unions have started to explore this route and indicates that this could shape the way trade unions are organised, structured and function in the future.

Chapter 2
Equality and Diversity and the Role of Trade Unions: Theoretical Approach

It is clear that the implementation and enforcement of anti-discrimination legislation on an individual level is not enough to tackle the multifaceted, deep rooted patterns of inequality experienced by some groups. There is a need to move beyond anti-discrimination policies designed to prevent unequal treatment of individuals (Commission of the European Communities 2005: 2).

Structural inequalities are part of our society and manifest themselves in the existing differences in social class, gender, ethnicity or nationality, religion, ability, sexual orientation, age to name but a few. At work such inequalities result in employment segregation and groups who face discrimination and prejudice are more likely to hold lower status and lower paid positions. As the above quote suggests, legislation and other policy interventions can address such inequalities to a certain extent but on their own they cannot tackle the embedded and prolonged social attitudes that contribute directly or indirectly to the discrimination faced by certain groups. Within this context it is important to look at the social processes that give rise to prejudice and discrimination but equally important to understand first, the general framework of challenging social inequalities and second, the role of social actors in this effort.

This chapter discusses the main theoretical debates on both the concepts of equality and of diversity, linking these to the role of trade unions and sets the context to understand the way the two concepts came to shape public policy and practice in Europe. In doing so we will look at the alternative approaches on individual and group difference, on equality of opportunity and on tackling social inequalities and at different models represented in the workplace to address the disadvantage and discrimination experienced by some social groups.

Background

There has been an increasing focus on equality and diversity in recent years and the terms came to be used together and often interchangeably in academic literature, policy making and in everyday life. Although the terms differ in their meaning and theoretical approach – equality being based on the concept of *sameness* while diversity is associated with the recognition of *difference* – both have been associated with the development of the equality discourse, as Healy et al. note, 'both same treatment and different treatment are required in order to deal with disadvantage that occurs due to different circumstances' (2010: 3) such as gender or disability. Furthermore, Thomson (2011) argues that a better understanding of difference and diversity is important for promoting and achieving equality.

Historically, the concept of equality in Europe had its roots in the moral and philosophical thinking of ancient Greece and the Enlightenment and is perceived as fundamental for democracy and the democratic values of 'liberty, equality, fraternity'. There is a spectrum of views on what equality is and the concept has evolved through different periods in history. It is beyond the purpose of this chapter and this book to review the philosophical arguments and the different approaches to equality but briefly in the area of work, as in education, according to Baker et al. (2004) the discussion on equality takes place in the form of an equal opportunities approach (also known as formal equality) which is well established in both academic debates and policy making. And it is this liberal egalitarian interpretation of equal opportunity that forms that basis of 'anti-discrimination legislation that makes it illegal to deny education or work to people because of their religion, sex or other specified characteristics' (Baker et al., 2004: 31). By mostly adopting the view of treating people as equals rather than treating people equally, this libertarian approach has been criticised for its failing to address the wider perspective of social inequality and power, such as for example the disparities in income and status (Squires, 2008).

Another criticism comes from those in favour of a more radical approach to equality, arguing not only for an equal opportunity but also for an equality of outcome (also known as substantive equality). Based on Rawl's principle of 'fair equality of opportunity' this argument entails the adoption of mechanisms to ensure not only fairer procedures for individuals to compete, fairly based on their strengths and talents but also for interventions at the workplace or in education in an effort to achieve a fairer distribution of outcomes (Baker et al., 2004). This approach is also known as affirmative action and the emphasis is on groups rather than the individual and as Phillips argues:

> ... it is more difficult to define equality of outcomes when we turn to comparisons between individuals rather than groups, but that the justified inequalities that arise from the exercise of individual choice form a much smaller category of inequalities ... where comparison between groups is concerned equality of outcome is much more pertinent as a measure of equality than is currently allowed (Phillips, 2004: 28).

One example is the adoption of quota systems or other preferential selection policies for women or ethnic minorities in the selection processes in education or the labour market to achieve better representation. European anti-discrimination legislation partially reflects both approaches as all Directives incorporate the concept of indirect discrimination but also provide for a measure of affirmative action which permits the adoption of certain preventative measures for groups that experience disadvantage (McCrudden, 2003).

A more recent approach is the concept of diversity which has been developed in the last 20 to 30 years, mainly in the US but gradually transferring to Europe and seen as the outcome of identity politics and the civil rights' movement in the 1960s, has increasingly been used to shape European policy and legislation. Hyman et al., (2012) identified five main reasons for the recognition and popularity of this approach. First, the systematic attention to gender related inequalities in the labour market. Although throughout history women have always worked – especially women from working class backgrounds – women remained a 'hidden' force in labour history as they were often excluded from some sectors while particularly targeted for others (Bradley, 1989). Continuous campaigning, changes in societal attitudes and in legislation led to a further increase of women entering the workplace and in a range of employment sectors while increasing the pace of demands to reduce discrimination based on gender differences, for example the campaign for equal pay which has a long history[1] in the UK and which has been a feature of trade union demands throughout Europe since at least the 1970s. Second the development of supranational anti-discrimination legislation by the European Union and the adoption of the Council Directive (2000/43/EC) on equal treatment irrespective of racial and ethnic origin and Council Directive (2000/78/EC) on equal treatment in employment and occupation[2] by Member States in order to make discrimination based on race or ethnicity, religion or belief, age, disability and sexual orientation unlawful at the workplace (ILO, 2007). Third there has been an increasing debate and awareness in contemporary European societies on persisting forms of discrimination such as for example ethnic minorities, lesbians and gays or disabled people. Fourth, as a result of globalisation there has been a steady increase in labour migration movements around the

---

1 The demand for Equal Pay in the UK can be first located in the 1830s and has continued throughout the nineteenth and twentieth centuries. For more information on the different stages of the campaign for Equal Pay see Mary Davis's 'Historical Introduction to the Campaign for Equal Pay' which can be found at http://www.unionhistory.info/equalpay/roaddisplay.php?irn=820 (accessed May 2014).

2 The two Council Directives, 2000/43/EC of 29 June 2000 implementing the principle of equal treatment between persons irrespective of racial or ethnic origin and Council Directive 2000/78/EC of 27 Nov. 2000 were introduced to establish an equal treatment in employment and occupation framework.

world. Within the European Union one of the fundamental rights is the free movement of people within the member states and despite the controversies and the attempts to tighten migration controls, there has been a visible movement of population for the purpose of work, study or retirement. Finally, there has been an argument for the *'business case'* for diversity, where employers or policy makers seek to focus on alternative models which draw on concepts of social integration and inclusion and which are advanced as being in contrast to equal opportunity policies that are mainly based on legislation.

In its current form the 'business case' has become the dominant approach of diversity and is mainly associated with management practices of introducing inclusive and non-discriminatory policies within organisations (Noon, 2007). According to business model research, emphasising individual differences can be essential for businesses today as they can boost creativity, provide a better understanding of the market needs and enhance performance and therefore provide an organisation with a cutting edge advantage to innovate and succeed in the increasingly competitive and global market (Roosevelt, 1990). Conceptually, as we will explore further in the next section, there is a tension between the business model and the equal opportunities model as the latter has been associated with a focus on equality and social justice.

Defining Equality and Diversity

There is no agreed definition of *equality* or *diversity* as both terms can acquire different meanings. The definitions used for the Mapping study were both EU related, either relevant to the EU legislation or to EU funded projects.

Accordingly, equality describes an approach that intends to ensure that people have an equal chance to participate in society, activities and services such as employment, education or healthcare. On the other hand the equal opportunities approach, as we see later, focuses on levelling the playing field, through measures such as the elimination of prejudices and processes that lead to discriminatory outcomes and through compensation for unfair disadvantages by means of public policies and any relevant private sector initiatives (such as for instance, those related to corporate social responsibility, the 'business case' for diversity and so on). This definition differs from the concept of formal equality which is more concerned with the consistent treatment of individuals who are alike and should be treated alike and not on the basis of their characteristics that are not objectively relevant in a given situation. On the other hand diversity in the area of employment has been defined[3]

3 This definition of 'diversity' is the same as that being used within the project 'Promoting diversity management in the workplace across the EU', funded by the EU

as a way of understanding, recognising and valuing people's differences and similarities, as they present enormous potential for an organisation as a source of innovation, problem-solving, customer orientation and many more (European Commission, 2010: 9).

Elements of each of these definitions are also reflected in the equality and diversity definitions provided by the Trade Union Congress (TUC) in the UK:

> Equality of opportunity is about ensuring everybody has an equal chance to take up opportunities and also to make full use of the opportunities on offer and to fulfil their potential' and 'Diversity is about celebrating and valuing how different we all are. This is strongly linked with promoting human rights and freedoms, based on principles such as dignity and respect. Diversity is about recognising, valuing and taking account of people's different backgrounds, knowledge, skills, and experiences, and encouraging and using those differences to create a productive and effective workforce.[4]

Although some commentators have argued that the simple distinction between 'sameness' and 'difference' that characterises the two concepts is useful in understanding disadvantage in contemporary society, others have looked to the approaches of equal opportunities and the 'business case' to highlight that there is an important difference between the two, as the first approach is based on a social justice argument while the latter is based on neoliberal management practices which have been put in place by modern management systems in order to ensure fairness within organisations by enhancing difference (Noon, 2007) but with the ultimate aim of becoming more competitive and of increasing profits for the organisations. Ozbilgin and Tatli (2011) note that the arguments in favour of diversity management being offered as an alternative to equal opportunities started to take shape during a period of a changing political and economic direction towards greater liberalisation and deregulation in US and the UK. Existing literature shows that there has been a range of explanations for the shift from equal opportunities to diversity management which also shows that this wider perspective of diversity can apply to more groups of people. For example, Kandola and Fullerton (1998) see diversity as a new paradigm that represents an alternative to equal opportunities where the focus is on the potential of each individual employee and the appreciation of the different experiences and perspectives that each individual employee brings to the work environment. And although the two authors do not reject the social justice aspect of equal opportunities, they see that the model of diversity management

---

Progress programme.

4 Unionlearn: http://www.unionlearn.org.uk/campaigns/equality-and-diversity/whats-difference (accessed in April 2014).

which places emphasis on individual characteristics can be advantageous for organisations in terms of competitiveness and future development (Kirton and Greene, 2010) but also allow for the opportunity for all to participate and develop their talent and career (Kandola and Fullerton, 1998). Others have highlighted an ambiguity between 'sameness' and 'difference' within the diversity management discourse and it can be argued that diversity management is a renewed or repackaged version of old equality and equal opportunities policies as a means of tackling discrimination in the workplace. For example Kamp and Hagedorn-Rasmussen found in their research that the introduction of diversity management in the Danish organisation they studied placed more emphasis on 'sameness' rather than 'difference', which is often associated with diversity management, while the integration of the ethnically diverse workforce took place through assimilation rather than 'plural multicultural organisation' (Kamp and Hagedorn-Rasmussen, 2004: 549). The two authors however attribute some of these trends to the work and influence of trade unions which is more prominent in the case of Europe than the US and which puts more emphasis on equality and 'sameness' (Kamp and Hagedorn Rasmussen, 2004).

There have been a number of criticisms of the diversity approach and the 'business case' and the main question asked is whether diversity management is good for equality. First the focus on individual differences rather than the collective group differences makes the approach both narrow and for some superficial. For example Nkomo (cited in Wrench, 2005) doubts that the individual approach of the 'business case' can effectively understand issues of race, gender and class within organisations:

> is diversity management really just about talking about respecting all individual differences? If so, this is problematic and cannot in its present form lead to inclusive organisations. There is a real danger in seeing differences as benign variation among people. It overlooks the role of conflict, power, dominance and the history of how organisations are fundamentally structured by race, gender and class (cited in Wrench 2005: 82).

And issues that relate to social inequalities, for example power relations, tend to be overlooked (Litvin, 2006; Noon, 2007). Nancy Fraser (1997) argues that questions of difference must not exclude social and economic exclusion or exclusion from power relations as despite the differences between socioeconomic injustice, and cultural injustice, they are both widespread in contemporary society.[5]

---

5 In what is called 'the redistribution–recognition dilemma' the American scholar Nancy Fraser argues that 'demands for 'recognition of difference' fuel struggles of groups mobilised under the banners of nationality, ethnicity, 'race', gender, and sexuality … Cultural domination supplants exploitation as the fundamental injustice. And cultural

This takes us to the second criticism of the oversimplified approach of diversity management: namely that it overlooks the complexity of socially constructed social divisions in society. Therefore according to Wrench (2005) despite the various schemes developed as part of the diversity management approach, such as training, mentoring and teamwork, 'the real problems of exclusion, conflict, harassment and marginalisation continue to exist in organisations' (Wrench, 2005: 80). Third, as mentioned above, some authors noted the connection of the 'business case' to market-related arguments for example, ofprofitability or business performance and questioned its ability to achieve social justice (Kaler, 2001). What happens for example in periods of economic crisis, as we shall discuss in Chapter 8, or what happens in cases where it is more profitable for a business to adopt unethical practices (Kaler, 2001)? Supporters of the moral argument (social justice approach) are sceptical of building diversity and equality policies on arguments of financial opportunity or advantage, as managerially-based solutions do not deliver equality in any meaningful way (Noon, 2007; Davies, 2003). Dickens (1997) indicates that although it is important for employers to be involved in promoting equality at the workplace they must be supported by policies aiming at a longer-term benefit both for their employees and the society as a whole. Equality should not be left to the voluntary action of employers who respond to market trends as this is often 'selective and partial with a different purchase in respect of different groups', for example prioritising gender over race (Dickens, 1997: 287). Furthermore employers are even more unlikely to improve working and pay conditions for part-time workers – the majority of whom are female – and this contributes to greater inequality in the labour market, as it widens the gender pay gap (Rubery et al., 1999).

Despite the criticism of the 'business case', diversity has been deemed as a useful tool to explain social difference and fight discrimination on various grounds, especially with regard to the 'sameness' and 'difference' arguments which see diversity as 'a barometer of societal inequalities', rather than 'good economic/business sense', as characterised by Acker (2007). 'United in diversity' which first came into use in 2000 has been the motto of the European Union and 'it signifies how Europeans have come together, in the form of the EU, to work for peace and prosperity, while at the same time being enriched by the continent's many different cultures, traditions and languages'.[6]

Thompson (2011) argues that difference can be viewed as a reaction to 'normalisation' and the imposition of social norms that act against diversity. And even in the 'business case' argument, Tomlinson and Schwabenland

---

recognition displaces socioeconomic redistribution as the remedy for injustice and the goal of political struggle' but for the author justice requires both redistribution and recognition (Fraser, 1997: 68).

6 http://europa.eu/about-eu/basic-information/symbols/motto/index_en.htm.

(2010) argue that researchers found that the 'business case' and social justice perspectives can coexist and achieve social equality, especially in voluntary sector organisations, many of whom originate in social movements for whom fighting for social justice has been the root of the existence. Further, Gedalof commenting on the *liberal notion of sameness* notes that:

> the privileging of sameness over difference results, not in the production of universal values, but rather in the effective universalising of the particular interests and perspectives of dominant groups (2013: 120).

Therefore, and quoting Young, difference should be viewed as a resource to better understand society, its divisions and its complexities under new lenses (Gedalof, 2013). In Chapter 7 we examine the case of multiple discrimination and the theoretical approach of intersectionality and we explore in more detail the complexities of group differences and equal opportunities and 'sameness' and 'difference' to better understand disadvantage and discrimination (Kirton and Green, 2006; Foster and Williams, 2010).

The Role of Trade Unions

Originating in the nineteenth century[7] and associated with the industrial revolution, most trade unions in Europe grew rapidly in the early twentieth century especially after the First World War. In a broad sense the primary objective of trade unions is to provide representation for workers. Trade unions are collective associations of workers formed to improve their ability to negotiate with employers over working conditions and rewards and, sometimes, to represent common interests within the political sphere beyond the workplace (Watson, 2008: 291). In the UK, the Trade Union and Labour Relations (Consolidation) Act 1992 defines a trade union as an organisation which consists wholly or mainly of workers of one or more descriptions and whose principal purposes include the regulation of relations between workers and employers or employers' associations. Commenting on this intermediary role, trade unions can be understood through four main relationships, according to Gumbrell-McCormick and Hyman (2013): with their own members to whom they are accountable; with the employers for issues of representation and work conditions; with government and policy making as part of the industrial relations in democratic processes; and with other civil society organisations

---

7 Although some trade unions have origins before the 19th century, before and during the period of the industrial revolution which prompted the conditions towards the establishment of collective organisation.

such as other non-governmental organisations (NGOs) that share a common purpose fighting discrimination. This latter aspect of trade union relationships is examined in Chapter 6 of this book.

Looking at the same issue, Ewing (2005) identified five main functions of the trade unions. First is the service function where trade unions provide services and benefits for their members. In a more contemporary sense this is the provision of legal advice, training or other benefits. Second is the representation function. This has both individual and collective characteristics, ranging from professional support and advocacy for individuals, to consultation or collective bargaining, on the behalf of the whole workforce. Third is the regulatory function where trade unions participate in Joint Industrial Councils (in some parts of the public sector) which set the terms and conditions for a sector or work to secure regulatory legislation. Fourth is the governmental and public administration function, where the trade unions engage with the government to secure legislation that is relevant to their activities and to perform their regulatory function. Finally, there is the public administration function, where trade unions are involved in the organised political representation of working people and in the development, implementation and delivery of public policies. It can be argued that these five relationships shape trade union activities in contemporary society.

In terms of equality and diversity, relevant literature highlights the commitment of trade unions to issues of equality and social justice (Dickens, 1999). Trade unions are also considered as most effective in fighting discrimination at work as they:

> have played a leading role in helping workers resist abuse … Along with higher wages and better benefits; protection from arbitrary management actions has been a central concern for trade unions. Unions protect workers from abuse through providing grievance procedures and through acting as ombudsmen for employees (Hodson, 2001: 102).

And Flanders sees a much deeper role for trade unions in protecting workers as protection is also about 'security, status and self-respect – in short their dignity as human beings' (1970: 21). Research has shown that in unionised workplaces workers are less likely to have their rights violated and they can also improve their work conditions (Brown et al., 2000; Colling, 2006).

But there have also been criticisms, mainly of the traditional structure and leadership of trade unions, for not adequately addressing the specific concerns of disadvantaged and minority groups, such as women or people from ethnic minorities (Kirton and Greene, 2006) resulting in their relative marginalisation. Indeed this has been a criticism throughout the history of trade unions where, for example, working women and later different ethnic groups have had to fight to be fully accepted as equal members of the mainstream unions.[8] A male-dominated 'discriminatory' environment, the traditional (masculine/ white) image of union leaders, traditional meeting procedures or union jargon all created a negative image amongst some members (and non-members). Conceptualising the role of women within union structures, Cockburn (1995) writes:

> The trade union reps that join the bureaucrats and businessmen on the weekday flights to Brussels have done little to dilute the grey-suited masculinity of the queue at the check in counter: the trade unionists too are all men (1995: 171).

Such inequality reflected of course the overall position of less represented groups within society as a whole. Lack of women officers and women in decision-making structures had a knock-on effect, and research has shown that women trade union representatives and officers did seek to make trade unions more 'women-friendly' (Heery and Kelly, 1988; Heery 2006) and to include discussions on equal pay, childcare, and the issue of enhancing the recruitment and participation of women. Equally, Jefferys and Ouali (2007), in a comparative study of racism in public transport trade unions in France, Belgium and the UK found that in cases where the majority of workers in local unions were white there was very little effort to combat institutional discrimination and that local unions did not put any pressure on management for equal representation of non-white workers. Despite these criticisms however research has also shown that women have enjoyed better pay and work conditions in unionised workplaces (Martin and Roberts, 1984) and that unionised workplaces are more likely to have well defined equality and diversities policies and practices than non-unionised ones (Kersley et al., 2006, Noon and Hoque, 2001).

In a Euro barometer survey *Discrimination in the EU in 2012*[9] respondents were asked where they would seek help if they became a victim of discrimination. A third of Europeans (34%) said that they would prefer to report their case to the police, 16% would report it to other organisations such as the equality bodies, 14% would approach a lawyer and 10% each would go to a tribunal or trade unions. These results are similar to the *Discrimination in the EU in 2009*[10] Euro barometer survey with the only difference that trade unions lost ground by 3%. However there is a great variation in responses across the different nations. For

---

8 An example to illustrate this point is the 'marriage bar' which prohibited married women to work which according to Hakim (2000) it the UK it was 'imposed and policed' by both the employers and the trade unions.

9 See also Chapter 3 (ec.europa.eu/public_opinion/archives/ebs/ebs_393_en.pdf)

10 ec.europa.eu/public_opinion/archives/ebs/ebs_317_en.pdf.

example in Denmark, Finland, Sweden, Belgium and the UK there was a higher percentage of respondents that would approach a trade union. Such variation may reflect the position of the union within a country; it may also reflect the trade unions' engagement with diversity issues, their publicity or membership (McKay, 2011). But the result may nevertheless suggest that despite increased activity by trade unions across Europe to promote equality, there is a general loss of the trade unions' public status (ibid.).

Parallel to that is the decreasing membership in trade union density across Europe. The European Industrial Relations Observatory (EIRO)[11] data of 22 EU countries shows that trade unions experienced a decrease in density levels in the period between 2003 and 2008: over 10 percentage points in Slovakia and Sweden; five to 10 points in Austria, Bulgaria, Denmark, Hungary, Latvia, Lithuania and Malta; one to five points in Cyprus, Estonia, Finland Germany, Ireland, Italy, the Netherlands, Norway and Slovenia; and under one percentage point in Portugal, Romania, Spain and the UK. In Central and Eastern European Countries (CEEC) trade union density is still decreasing, however the rate of decrease has slowed down when compared with the previous period 1993–2003. In countries where trade union membership increased in the period 2003–2008, union density has in fact decreased because the absolute number of employees rose by more. These include Cyprus, Finland, Ireland, Italy, Norway, Portugal, Romania, Slovenia and the UK. In Austria, Bulgaria, Denmark, Estonia, Germany, Hungary, Latvia, Malta, Slovakia and Sweden trade union membership fell despite a rise in employee numbers (EIRO, 2009).[12] There have been a range of explanations for trade union density decrease, some are country specific but some reflect more general trends in European societies. These include the introduction of neoliberal policies, with the emphasis on the individual rather than the collective; the disengagement of younger people with trade unions; the increase of precarious and casual forms of employment in workplaces with limited access to trade union representation; as well as the economic crisis and the rising number of unemployed workers. But the market economy is also considered a major factor as increasingly trade unions are being marginalised as Brown and Marsden note:

---

11 The European Industrial Relations Observatory (EIRO) was established in 1997 by the European Foundation for the Improvement of Living and Working Conditions and offers news and analysis on European industrial relations. It is an instrument that collects, analyses and disseminates up-to-date information in the area of industrial relations in Europe and serves the needs of national and European level organisations of the social partners, governmental organisations and EU institutions (http://www.eurofound.europa.eu/eiro/structure.htm, accessed in June 2014).

12 http://www.eurofound.europa.eu/eiro/studies/tn0904019s/tn0904019s.htm.

firm by firm and sector by sector, employers have responded to tougher competition by tightening controls over work, and either refusing to deal with trade unions at all or doing so only on the basis that their role is one of passive consultation or of positive contribution to improved productivity (2010: 3).

Despite their declining membership, trade unions are considered as key social actors in European social dialogue. In fact, as we see in Chapter 3, the two European Directives (Council Directive (2000/43/EC) and Council Directive (2000/78/EC)) impose specific obligations on trade unions to:

take adequate measures to promote social dialogue between the two sides of industry with a view to fostering equal treatment, including through the monitoring of workplace practices, collective agreements, codes of conduct, research or exchange of experiences and good practices (McKay, 2011).

Trade unions are a membership type of organisations, rooted in the workforce and accountable to their members; however according to Fulton (2010) they are also organisations with the capacity to play an integral part in social dialogue depending on their resources and the support of their members.

Trade Union Practices on Anti-discrimination and Diversity

The following section provides some examples from the Mapping research on trade union practices across Europe and shows how some of the concepts discussed above have materialised in trade union policies. To recap, the study aimed to identify significant and innovative initiatives on anti-discrimination and diversity in five different discrimination strands as identified by the European Council Directives: race/ethnic origin, disability, sexual orientation, age and religion/belief. The Mapping study did not include gender as a specific discrimination strands, as gender was mainstreamed in the study (see Chapter 3). As we have seen in the introductory chapter, the study was based on more than 250 in-depth face-to-face interviews with trade union senior representatives in 34 European states, as well as with representatives of around 70 NGOs exploring their views, perceptions and understandings of the two European Council Directives.

The Mapping study found that in most countries trade unions had adopted measures at local, national, cross-country and European levels to combat discrimination. In particular it was observed that trade unions in 29 out of the 34 countries participating in the study, took the following forms of action: adopted new ways of organisation; changed their structures to encourage participation and self-organisation; adopted specific budgets in relation to their equality agenda; took concentrated action to increase the numbers of members or union activists from discriminated groups; and adopted self-organisation. In addition the data from the Mapping study also included references to diversity management and the 'business case' for diversity. As an analytical tool the study divided the initiatives into two categories, significant and innovative. This enabled a better understanding of the available anti-discrimination initiatives in terms of their contribution to eliminating discrimination but also the union processes themselves in responding to the new trends, dictated by the legislative changes through the European directives and any challenges these might have caused to their structures. As 'significant' the study defined those trade union initiatives that had a wide coverage, were likely to be sustained (or repeated if they were one-off initiatives) or were important in the national context in which the initiative took place. Initiatives that represented new ways of engagement for the trade union, in the context in which it operated or in engagement beyond traditional trade union communities were included in the 'innovative' category of initiatives.[13]

The initiatives studied included projects on both direct and indirect discrimination, again another feature of the European Council Directives. Direct discrimination occurs when a person is treated less favourably than another is, has been or would be treated in a comparable situation, on the grounds of religion or belief, disability, age, sexual orientation or racial/ethnic origin with regards to employment and occupation. Indirect discrimination on the other hand occurs where an apparently neutral provision, criterion or practice would put persons having a particular religion or belief, or particular disability, particular age, a particular sexual orientation or a particular racial or ethnic origin at a disadvantage compared to other people. Unless this provision is objectively justified it is treated as a form of discrimination.

New Ways of Organisation

Unions across Europe had developed projects and initiatives that related to new ways of organising workers, including those from minority groups. Some of the initiatives encompassed undertaking research surveys in order to gather more information, explore the views and perceptions of the relevant minority groups and assess the needs of these groups. One example was a practice developed by the Italian Union of Labour (UIL) union to combat discrimination on the ground of race/ethnicity. The project 'Speech to migrants' (La parola agli immigrati) involved employers and migrant workers responding to a common questionnaire on the topic of migrants and discrimination at workplace.

---

13 *Trade union practices on antidiscrimination and diversity, 2010, Final report.*

Other initiatives were based on the organisation of specific campaigns. Examples included the 'badge campaign' by the Icelandic Confederation of Labour (ASI) aimed at raising awareness and supporting different ethnicities, inside and outside the workplace but with a strong focus on equality, as helping defend good working conditions for all workers. This involved a badge with the inscription 'I'm learning Icelandic, I speak five languages', or 'I speak a little bit of Icelandic'. This campaign was developed in conjunction with another campaign on employment rights, 'One right no cheating' which was aimed at defending the working conditions of all workers. An innovative poster on multiple levels of discrimination was created by the youth group of the German public sector trade union, Verdi, which depicted a head composed of two halves, one white, one black, meaning that every person is human irrespective of race or colour, as the trade union interviewee in the Mapping study noted 'this was a visual expression of our position/our claim intended to hit other people's minds'.

Finally, another new form of organising involved the provision of special services by the trade unions to disadvantaged and marginalised groups. The Italian Union of Labour (UIL) provided special services to women, migrants and younger people that faced problems not only in workplaces but also in their lives in general. In particular, there had been a reported increase in the number of cases brought to the court because for an increasing numbers of workers, their employment contract did not protect them adequately.

Structural Changes to Encourage Participation

Structural changes involved either changing or creating new structures within the union in order to promote better representation for minority groups and as a strategy to increase membership numbers. This action could take a variety of forms. In some cases it entailed changes in the voting systems, as in the case of the CNV Education union in the Netherlands (CNVO) the trade union interviewee to the Mapping study provided an example of an innovative project adopted by the union:

> in the general union meeting a new voting structure has been designed to enable women's votes to weigh more. Most of the active members are men who attend such meetings. To make sure that women's interests are being respected this voting system has been designed (Netherlands, trade union interviewee).

In some cases the union had created affiliated centres to target specific groups, for example in Sweden at a local level, the Commercial Workers Union (Handels) took a significant initiative and established a centre for supporting undocumented workers in Stockholm in 2008 to fight xenophobia and racism against foreign workers. In Italy the Italian General Confederation of

Labour (CGIL) created a 'New rights' desk to provide direct help to victims of discrimination while the United Federation of Danish Workers (3F union) in Denmark had created a dedicated 'equality unit'. Other cases involved the appointment of representatives or the establishment of reserved seats from specific groups – a more proactive move towards positive action. For example in Austria the Youth Organisation of the Austrian Federation of Trade Unions (OEGJ) had appointed youth representatives to the executive board with voting rights. Examples of structural changes had also been referred to as representing pioneering work in countries where stereotypes for particular groups were more pronounced; for example, in Poland the All-Poland, Alliance of Trade Unions (OPZZ) had established the post of Lesbian and Gay Bisexual and Transgendered (LGBT) officer as means of fighting homophobia in the Polish society and of opposing prejudices against minority groups.

Specific Budgets in Relation to their Equality Agenda

To understand the extent of their equality commitment, trade union participants were asked if they had specific budgets for promoting equality through their organisation. There was limited evidence that trade unions had dedicated budgets for equality and antidiscrimination work although some of the initiatives mentioned had only materialised because of the financial support from the trade union. Examples included workshops organised by unions or the appointment of officers with a specific equality function (McKay, 2011).

Unions also expressed their frustration with the lack of finances to support what they considered vital causes for the whole society. For example a trade union representative in Greece from the Federation of Secondary School Teachers (OLME) noted that the teacher training programmes on multiculturalism could not be materialised as there was a considerable lack the resources and/ or capacity. As the interviewee pointed out, the government was well aware of these demands but only limited or no action was taken:

> but now in the last ten years it appears that the whole programme of training
> for teachers does not function adequately. However one positive step is that in
> other education-related subjects there is a course on multiculturalism (Greece,
> trade union interviewee).

Action to Increase the Number of Members or Union Activists from Discriminated Groups

Having a dedicated union representative at the workplace has been one of the key roles of the trade unions. The existence of activists specially trained on

23

issues of equality and anti-discrimination who directly interact with members (and non-members) and in particular with members from minority groups could be also considered another trade union function. Only a few examples were reported to the Mapping study. One related to age discrimination (young workers) and was from the Youth Organisation of the Austrian (OEGJ): the creation of a youth representative post within companies who functioned as mediators between employees and company managers. The interviewee explained that if a company employed five or more young people or apprentices, one youth representative could be elected to represent the cultural, social and political interests of the young staff within the company. She or he could take up to two weeks of paid leave for further training as a youth representative and could evoke a youth assembly to inform young employees. If problems with one of the apprentices arose within a company, the youth representative had to be informed and involved in the consultation as to what would happen to the young person in question. The youth representative had an important role as mediator with an understanding of any problems young employees were confronted with and to mediate between the young people and the managers.

Another example can be drawn from a quota system where Samis, the Norwegian minority ethnic group, were represented in the Utdanningsforbundet (educational association) through, reserved seats. The Union of Education in Norway (UEN) was working to ensure that all Sami students in Norway were taught the Sami language, as well as Sami history and culture. The union promoted the Sami population's rights to learn their own language and culture through having representatives in the trade union with a particular focus on the three different Sami-languages.

Other examples involved the appointment of migrant workers to representative posts in the trade unions. In Belgium the General Federation of Belgian Labour (FGBT) union encouraged migrants to run for the positions as workers' representatives in companies, with a Belgian union respondent reporting that at its 2009 inter-union forum on diversity 250 union representatives were present, whereas three years previously there was a handful of shop stewards and officials who were sufficiently concerned to attend. And in Austria the regional organisation of the Austrian Federation of Trade Unions (OGB-OO) had encouraged workers' representatives with migrant backgrounds to run as workers' representatives in companies, recognising a situation in Upper Austria where 12% of the workforce did not have Austrian citizenship and 18% were workers from migrant background at the time of the Mapping study

Self-organisation

Debate has been generated about the self-organisation of minority groups. Healy and Kirton (2000) show that there has been a shift in the UK in the

1990s towards greater separate organisation; other relevant literature highlights the controversy and academic debates on the concept (see for example Wrench and Virdi, 1996). Moore and Wright, in their research into the model of equality representatives in the UK, argued that this differs from the self-organisation model, mainly because the former is based on a more liberal notion of fairness and equality while the latter is based on a more radical approach of difference such as gender or race (Moore and Wright, 2012). Their study found that Equality Representatives (ERs) came into existence in a period of more individualistic responses to workplace inequalities, such as through an individual grievance process at the expense of collective action but found ERs to be part of a more inclusive and transformational approach to equality at the level of the workplace and organisation (2012: 445)

Equally self-organisation has been considered an effective way of organising in challenging trade union bureaucracies. The Mapping study found some examples of self-organisation as a method for trade unions to address issues of equality and diversity. For example, in Ireland, the Irish National Teachers' Organisation (INTO) union had established a self-organised LGBT group which had first intervened at the union's 2007 conference, addressing it on dignity at work in terms of sexual orientation. This group was believed to be a valuable part of the union and the union's 37,000 members had become more supportive as the group had become more visible, for example, in the previous five years the president of the union had participated in Gay Pride march alongside the LGBT group.

Managing Diversity, the 'business case'

Despite the debate and tensions between the concepts of equality and diversity, especially the 'business case' approach which was discussed in the first part of this chapter, the Mapping study found that many initiatives developed by the trade unions did focus on diversity at work usually within the context of social dialogue. For example the National Federation of Christian Trade Unions (CNV) interviewee in Netherlands discussed the union's participation in a research project named 'Ethnic diversity as success'. This was a study into company practices within various companies, which were trying to use ethnic diversity as a key for success and who stressed that this was the case in various sectors (insurance, employment agency, supermarkets, cleaning and youth care). With this project CNV aimed to contribute to more effective Collective Labour Agreements and to stimulate the participation of ethnic minorities. This was considered as a useful strategy to improve bargaining and member participation. Other unions in France, Belgium, Netherlands and Spain discussed their diversity strategies mainly in relation to ethnic diversity, disability and age (focusing on young people).

Conclusion

The chapter conceptualised the two important concepts of this book, equality and diversity and the two approaches associated with them, equal opportunities and the 'business case' for managing diversity. It has been argued that equality and equal opportunities have a longer history in philosophical and political thought than diversity, and especially the 'business case' which became popular in the 1970s and 1980s during a period of deregulation and the introduction of an increasingly neoliberal economic system. In terms of social change this was a period where social thinking concentrated on identity politics and the way this has been articulated in the equality and diversity debate is the division between the ideas of 'sameness' and 'difference', or collective and individualistic responses. And this is the approach that has influenced the current social thinking, the economic system on a global scale and the national and supranational politics in terms of equality and diversity.

Trade unions in most of the EU Member States supported equality, equal opportunities and social justice practices as a matter of principle but at the same time, also due to the greater demographic diversity, globalisation and pressure from members. We have noted instances where they had adjusted their policies to take account of new developments. The second part of the chapter considered the two concepts within the trade union framework and also presented some of the Mapping study research findings as examples of how equality and diversity concepts have been articulated through initiatives that aim to reduce discrimination. The following chapters will discuss some of the findings from the Mapping study in more detail.

Chapter 3
Grounds of Discrimination

Europe is currently undergoing a prolonged process of rapid intergroup changes. The responses to this sweeping transformation have included prejudice, discrimination and violence as well as acceptance and cultural enrichment. Such a massive and important phenomenon deserves intensive social scientific study for what we can learn as well as for what we can contribute to the continent's future harmony and social justice (Zick et al., 2008).

This chapter looks at wider issues of disadvantage and discrimination in the labour market where particular social groups may face negative stereotyping and exclusion, taking Zick et al.'s call that the subject deserves further study. It does this through an exploration of the role of legislation at European level, specifically at the two key European Directives[1] and the protection they provide for the different strands of discrimination – race and ethnicity, age (young and old), disability, sexual orientation and religion or belief. It offers a critique of this legislative approach while also investigating the potential of the law to affect changes in the workplace and, in particular, the behaviours of key workplace actors. Through the trade union agendas that incorporate equality and diversity, the chapter discusses the role of the existing European level legislation in tackling discrimination.

Article 1 of Directive 2000/78 (the equality directive) states that it applies on the 'grounds of religion or belief, disability, age or sexual orientation, as regards employment and occupation, with a view to putting into effect in the Member States the principle of equal treatment'. Article 1 of Council Directive 2000/43 (the race equality directive) lays down a framework for combating discrimination on the grounds of racial or ethnic origin, also with a view to putting into effect in the Member States the principle of equal treatment. Thus five grounds of discrimination are covered by the Directives, which both promote the principle of equal treatment and the concept of 'no less favourable treatment' on the basis of any of the grounds covered.

---

1 Council Directive 2000/43/EC of 29 June 2000 on implementing the principle of equal treatment between persons irrespective of racial or ethnic origin; Council Directive 2000/78/EC of 27 November 2000 establishing a general framework for equal treatment in employment and occupation.

Employment has always represented 'an important condition for social inclusion and independent living' (Kosa, 2013) but despite this there is a perception that discrimination in employment is more widespread than in other areas of life (Kosa, 2013). While an assessment of all of the available evidence demonstrates that Europe is now generally more tolerant than in the past, suggesting that equality legislation could have played a part, either by changing practices or perceptions or by influencing key actors, as we argue, legislation alone is rarely enough to produce significant change. Without the activities of key actors, including the trade unions, the improvements which we document would not have taken place. In support of this contention we can refer to the special Eurobarometer surveys undertaken at the request of the European Commission. These were conducted in 2007, 2009 and 2012 (European Commission, 2012),[2] providing consistent and comparable data which allows us to track changes in perceptions as to the levels of discrimination faced by workers in minority groups within the EU. The most recent Eurobarometer 2012 survey confirms that discrimination is still considered to be widespread within the EU, in particular on the grounds of ethnic origin, disability and sexual orientation, with more than half the Eurobarometer respondents (56%) stating this to be the case in relation to ethnicity. However, while it is of continuing concern that a majority still holds this view, the percentage responding in this way has fallen from the nearly two in three (64%) who held that view in 2007. Thus, while this does not provide grounds for complacency it does show that Europe is becoming more tolerant. Additionally, higher proportions, than in 2009, said that they 'would feel comfortable, rather than uncomfortable, if a person from a minority group were to lead the country. Of all minority groups, it is the Roma, who represent Europe's largest ethnic minority, that are believed to be most at risk of discrimination, with three out of four Eurobarometer respondents in 2012 stating this to be the case. This is based on an acknowledged reality of discrimination against the Roma, particularly in the field of employment, where fewer than one in three Roma are employed while, according to a submission from Amnesty International to the European Commission, half had been victims of discrimination on the grounds of ethnicity in the previous 12 months (Amnesty International, 2013). Moreover, demonstrating that these levels of prejudice also extend beyond the workplace, one in two Eurobarometer respondents reported that in their view their country's citizens would be 'uncomfortable or fairly uncomfortable' if their children had Roma schoolmates. These levels of prejudice are indicative of the size of the problem which the trade unions must confront in taking up issues of discrimination, not just on behalf of their members, but potentially in opposition to the views of at least some elements of their memberships.

---

2 See also Chapter 2.

Turning to the other strands of discrimination, Eurobarometer suggested that there were greater degrees of prejudice in the case of older persons, transgendered or transsexual persons, young people as well as those from a minority ethnic group. In contrast Europe's citizens expressed themselves as being more comfortable with the notion of a female leader or with someone who had a disability. Thus, while all the strands of discrimination appear equal within the directives, it is clear that, in relation to some areas, the challenge of combatting discrimination is higher than in others.

Just as the Roma are identified as a group largely excluded from the labour market, so too are those with disabilities who also have lower employment participation rates compared to the rates for workers without disabilities. Disability experts argue that the data concerning disability is too unreliable to make accurate assessments of the extent of discrimination, but are agreed that there is endemic discrimination against those who are disabled. This may not be demonstrated in overt forms but in the ways in which society is structured so that the disabled often appear invisible in the public arena, as an expert reporting to the Mapping study noted:

> Disabled people are still at significant disadvantage in the labour market in all European countries … They have, in general, lower participation rates, higher levels of unemployment and a lower educational attainment level, than the rest of the population. Most countries pursue active strategies to include and integrate people with disabilities in the labour market. However the degree of success is not always measured or evaluated.

Age discrimination in relation to recruitment and retention presents problems to Europe's older workers, as AGE Europe notes:

> It is therefore clear that age is fast becoming the most commonly perceived disadvantage in the labour market. This strongly reflects the reality that is faced by many older workers, in particular older women, who are among those most affected by the crisis and one of the groups most likely to lose their job and be unable to find new employment (Age Platform Europe, 2013).

One in six Eurobarometer respondents reported personal experience of discrimination, with those with a disability or belonging to a sexual or ethnic minority being likely to do so. One in three respondents had themselves witnessed or had heard of someone who had suffered discrimination in the previous year. This means that when addressing discrimination it is important to take account not just of those who may directly experience discrimination but also to recognise that discriminatory actions have a ripple effect. They create instability and uncertainty, particularly in employment, in those cases where discriminatory conduct is not successfully challenged.

We argue throughout this book that it is not just the case that the trade unions ought to have a major role in combating discrimination but that if they are absent there may be no challenge to discriminatory practices at work. One reason for this is the lack of knowledge of how to take discrimination claims. According to the Eurobarometer data, as we saw in Chapter 2, only one in three respondents knew where they should go if they were victims of discrimination. Where they did indicate knowledge, the police was the most likely group identified. This suggests first that there are few channels of support that individuals feel they can turn to when in need; however, it also suggests that discrimination is in some way associated with criminal behaviour and this could impact negatively on a willingness to challenge discriminatory actions where the consequences are to criminalise behaviours. Interestingly Eurobarometer suggests that there is a difference in perception of where the organs of support might be located, dependent on whether or not an individual is from a minority group and here there is less likelihood that individuals will refer their claim to the police. This may reflect a reality which is that those experiencing discrimination mainly want it to stop and this may represent their aims in pursuing the claim, rather than the desire for punitive sanctions. However, given that the police are the main group from whom support is sought, decisions not to refer cases to them also mean that victims have a narrower range of potential support channels.

Stereotypes, Prejudice and Discrimination

Prejudice and discrimination is a widespread phenomenon across Europe (Zick et al., 2008) and it feeds on stereotypes. Even in those Member States commonly viewed as tolerant, prejudice and stereotyping is still persistent, so that, for example, a recent study in Sweden found that discrimination on the basis of sexual orientation was still evident (Ahmet et al., 2013). Wagner, Christ and Pettigrew (2008), (cited in Zick et al.) demonstrate that prejudice is 'an important predictor of both avoiding of ethnic minorities as well as of aggressive behaviour intentions against these out-group members. Those who are considered as different are reconstructed around a stereotypical notion of who they are and how they will think and act' (2008: 246). AGE Platform notes:

> Most studies proved that employers' ageist attitudes were based on a combination of unfounded clichés about older workers' productivity and adaptability, as well as on some labour law and social protection provisions which indeed made older workers less attractive for employers (2013: 2).

This is confirmed in the Eurobarometer (2012) survey which found that older age and looks were most widely seen as factors that could put applicants at a disadvantage. At the same time 'every stereotypical assumption about older people, however, is also likely to be a stereotypical assumption about younger people' such as that:

> Soft skills are an important factor in the recruitment of young people. It may be that the judgments of these soft skills are more likely to be subject to stereotypical assumptions than more objective criteria such as qualifications or technical skills (Sargeant, 2013: 12).

However, what we also know is that the best way to challenge stereotyping and prejudice is by breaking down the barriers between minority and majority groups and we argue that not just is this the primary responsibility of the majority group, but that it also should be a priority for Europe's trade unions, if they are to combat prejudice and discrimination. An example which shows how this is the most effective way of challenging discriminatory attitudes can also be found in Eurobarometer which, while finding that Roma people are the most likely subjects of prejudice and stereotyping, reported that Europeans with Roma friends were more likely to give positive ratings of Roma, while membership of an ethnic minority also made respondents slightly less likely to be critical, than other minorities, in relation to their view of Roma peoples. Experiencing discrimination, either directly or indirectly though knowing others who have experienced it themselves, makes Europe's citizens more tolerant and readier to challenge stereotypes.

The Content of the EU Directives

From its establishment the European Union has committed itself to equality principles. The Treaty on European Union (Art. 6(1)) states that the Union is founded 'on the principles of liberty, democracy, respect for human rights and fundamental freedoms, and the rule of law, principles which are common to the Member States. Art. 6(2) furthermore states that the Union 'shall respect fundamental rights'. The principle of equal treatment as between women and men was established under Community law by way of Directive 76/207/ EEC of 9 February 1976 'On the implementation of the principle of equal treatment for men and women as regards access to employment, vocational training and promotion, and working conditions'. Action on the other non-discrimination strands took a lot longer to achieve and it was not until 1995 that the European Commission presented a communication on racism, xenophobia and anti-Semitism and in 1996 the Council of Ministers adopted a joint action 'to combat racism and xenophobia' under which Member States would undertake to ensure effective judicial cooperation in respect of offences based on racist or xenophobic behaviour. A directive was then proposed at the meeting of the European Council in Tampere in October 1999, with its legal basis found in Article 13 of the Treaty establishing the European Community, which states:

> Without prejudice to the other provisions of this Treaty and within the limits of the powers conferred by it upon the Community, the Council, acting unanimously on a proposal from the Commission and after consulting the European Parliament, may take appropriate action to combat discrimination based on sex, racial or ethnic origin, religion or belief, disability, age or sexual orientation.

Employment guidelines agreed by the Council in December 1999 stressed the need to 'foster conditions for a socially inclusive labour market by formulating a coherent set of policies aimed at combating discrimination against groups such as ethnic minorities'.

Two directives set out the legal framework for non-discrimination within the EU. Council Directive 2000/43/EC (the race equality directive) on implementing the principle of equal treatment between persons irrespective of racial or ethnic origin came into force on 29 June 2000 and was soon followed by Council Directive 2000/78/EC of 27 November 2000 (the equality directive) establishing a general framework for equal treatment in employment and occupation. The field of implementation for both directives is employment although, in relation to race equality, the Directive extends its competence to other aspects of daily life, such as education and social services. Combined the Directives cover all of the strands of discrimination, other than sex equality, which is treated by way of mainstreaming. Thus in tackling any of the grounds, account has also to be taken of the gender impact of any actions. The Mapping study also adopted a mainstreaming approach which we have carried forward into this book. Thus rather than interrogating sex discrimination as a separate strand, we investigate the approaches of trade unions and the extent to which they mainstream sex discrimination, in the context of their actions on the other grounds. Both directives reference other international and European standards, including the Universal Declaration of Human Rights, the UN Convention on the Elimination of All forms of Discrimination against Women and the Community Charter of Fundamental Social Rights which states:

> Any discrimination based on any ground such as sex, race, colour, ethnic or social origin, genetic features, language, religion or belief, political or any other

opinion, membership of a national minority, property, birth, disability, age or sexual orientation shall be prohibited.

Over the more than ten years since the implementation of the two Directives the approaches which the courts have adopted in their scrutiny of the principle of equal treatment have generally been similar across all strands, save in relation to disability where the nature of the discrimination and the method of assessing compensation has promoted a different approach which Greve has categorised as leading to 'a certain convergence in legal rights-based approaches' with 'some evidence of a shift from inactivity compensation towards assessments of capacity for work' (2009: 4).

The Role of the Social Partners in the Context of the Directives

A key point which we explore in this chapter is the extent to which the directives promote the social partners as relevant actors in relation to equality of treatment. In particular, since the focus of the book is on trade union actions and responses to instances of less favourable treatment, our aim is to highlight both the role and the actions of trade unions. The Eurobarometer 2012 survey notes that the proportion of individuals who would contact a trade union if they became a victim of discrimination or harassment fell by three percentage points between 2009 and 2012. This is unsurprising; trade unions in most EU countries have lost support in recent years, where support is measured through density levels or collective bargaining coverage. But the fall in the number of trade union members is not in itself an indication of a reduced role for the trade unions as social partners. As an examination of the Directives demonstrates, the social partners collectively have major responsibility for the effective implementation of equality and non-discrimination, limited only by those regulatory measures established under national law or practice. Both Directives give a key role to employers and trade unions (the social partners) for the elimination of discrimination and the promotion of equality of treatment. This key role establishes that the trade unions have legitimate interests beyond their involvement in collective bargaining, as the Preamble to Council Directive 2000/43 states:

> Member States should promote dialogue between the social partners and with non-governmental organisations to address different forms of discrimination and to combat them' (para. 23) .... [and that they may] .... 'entrust management and labour, at their joint request, with the implementation of this Directive as regards provisions falling within the scope of collective agreements, provided

that the Member States take all the necessary steps to ensure that they can at all times guarantee the results imposed by this Directive (para 28).

Council Directive 2000/78/EC acknowledges a similar role for the social partners, with an additional proviso that this should be 'within the framework of national practice'. The wording of both Directives is very similar, although in one the term used is 'social partners' whereas in the other it is 'management and labour'. It is not clear why there should be a difference and with regard to their interpretation the meanings appear to be interchangeable. There are also some other minor differences in their wording. Council Directive 2000/43/EC refers to the need to take 'any necessary steps' that promote equality, while Council Directive 2000/78/EC refers to 'all the necessary steps' to ensure that the results required by the Directives are guaranteed.

Social partner engagement is also encouraged and supported by European level NGOs. AGE Platform (2013) asserts that promotional campaigns and awareness-raising can best be achieved 'through investment in independent equality bodies working in partnership with a wide range of actors, including NGOs *and with a genuine contribution from social partners*'. Greve (2009) has expressed a similar position in relation to mainstreaming disability in employment policies, stating that the integration of the social partners in such policies is essential, given that implementation is best achieved at the local level so that 'social dialogue and involvement of the partners as part of the mainstreaming strategy can be very important' (2009: 19) particularly in advocating and informing about mainstreaming.

The role accorded to the social partners extends beyond their responsibility for collective agreements. First, the Directives specifically apply to membership of, and involvement in, an organisation of workers or employers or any organisation whose members carry on a particular profession, including the benefits provided for by such organisations (Art.1(1)(d) and Art. 3(1(d) respectively). The means that trade unions are under a specific legal obligation not to discriminate in the context of their activities. Furthermore the Directives establish that trade unions may also have 'a legitimate interest' in ensuring that the provisions of the Directives are complied with and, in line with national law, and provide that they may, with the approval of the individual making a complaint of difference in treatment, 'engage, either on behalf or in support of the complainant' (Art. 7(2) and Art 9(2) respectively).

Those elements which reinforce the role of the social partners relate to social dialogue (Art. 11 and Art. 13 respectively) and to compliance and implementation. Here a legal obligation (in accordance with national traditions and practice) is placed on Member States to:

take adequate measures to promote the social dialogue between the two sides of industry with a view to fostering equal treatment, including through the monitoring of workplace practices, collective agreements, codes of conduct, research or exchange of experiences and good practices.

to encourage the two sides of industry without prejudice to their autonomy to conclude, at the appropriate level, agreements laying down anti-discrimination rules ... in the fields ... . which fall within the scope of collective bargaining.

Furthermore implementation of the Directives can be entrusted to management and labour 'at their joint request' ... . 'as regards provisions falling within the scope of collective agreements'. The provisions do not give the social partners unchecked authority. They may not reach agreements which would be in breach of the aims of the Directives and, on the basis of Art 1(2) of the European Social Charter, any provision in a collective agreement which is contrary to the principle of equal treatment must be declared null and void or be rescinded, abrogated or amended. Art. 14(b) and Art. 16(b) respectively oblige Member States to take any necessary measures where 'provisions contrary to the principle of equal treatment' are 'included in individual or collective contracts or agreements' and any such provisions can be declared null and void or be amended. Thus the Directives face two ways; they both encourage social partner engagement while at the same time negating any such engagement where the outcome offends against the principle of no less favourable treatment.

The Directives also give a specific role to non-governmental organisations (NGOs) in so far as they encourage the involvement of NGOs, together with trade unions, to support the promotion of equal treatment. Art. 12 of Council Directive 2000/43/EC and Art. 14 of Council Directive 2000/78/EC make it clear that there is an obligation on Member States to encourage social dialogue 'with appropriate non-governmental organisations which have, in accordance with their national law and practice, a legitimate interest in contributing to the fight against discrimination on grounds of racial and ethnic origin, with a view to promoting the principle of equal treatment.

Trade unions, as associations or legal entities, are also empowered 'to engage in proceedings' such as are determined by Member States 'either on behalf or in support of any victim (paras 23 and 29). This signals that trade unions have the legal competence, where national law does not prohibit it, to have audience in the courts. Chopin and Uyen Do (2012) found that, in a range of Member States, there was express provision to that effect, so that within the EU only Finland and the UK did not permit this. In 15 Member States the right goes further and permits the trade unions, where they are in acting in the public interest, to take cases, even where there is no specified victim to support. However, in 11 Member States: Belgium, Cyprus, the Czech Republic, Estonia,

Finland, Greece, Ireland, Latvia, Luxembourg, Sweden and the UK that the right does not apply.

It is without question that the trade unions should be well-placed to promote equality since they will have direct knowledge of cases or potential cases of discrimination. Their involvement can therefore extend beyond providing information on the content of the Directives to providing support for victims of discrimination. There are also questions of competence, in relation to the complex legal issues that are often connected with claims[3] and these, combined with the cost of taking claims and the high risk of failure in most discrimination claims, undermines the potential of trade union involvement. Furthermore, there is widespread support within Europe for intervention within the workplace to combat discrimination. According to Eurobarometer 2012, 79% of respondents support employer-provided training, 76% support the monitoring of recruitment procedures and 69% support monitoring the composition of the workforce.

Case study example A

This example draws on data from the Netherlands Federation of Christian Trade Unions (CNV) and was the basis for one of the Mapping case studies. The case study was based on three major initiatives taken by the union on ethnic diversity, age discrimination (in relation to young workers) and discrimination against young disabled workers. The initiatives led directly to social partner engagement on the issue of non-discrimination and produced several identifiable outcomes which were seen as combatting discrimination.

The first of the initiatives had its origin in a research project *Ethnic diversity for success* which was aimed at improving the labour market position of minority ethnic workers and which had collected good practice examples and had examined collective agreements to identify those measures which led to measureable improvements. The research was able to demonstrate that the participating companies had benefited from having a more diverse workforce and at the same time it encouraged the union to be itself more proactive in demanding that employers address inequality at work.

At about the same time the youth wing of the trade union had begun to campaign against the issue of temporary contracts to young workers in

---

3 For example, the European Disability Forum, in its document *Evaluating the 'Defence of rights' under the Employment Directive* (April 2013) notes that while there is a key role for the trade unions, 'they do not always have expertise in disability'.

supermarkets and their campaign encouraged co-operative working between two trade unions, the CNV and the FNV (the Federation of Dutch Trade Unions). The workers argued that the contractual position of supermarket workers was a consequence of their age and that the supermarkets were offering temporary contracts simply because the workers were young. The union then took a test case to a tribunal and won. This led to a lot of media attention but also led to larger numbers of young workers choosing to join the union. It also contributed to a greater awareness of age discrimination, particularly as it operates in relation to young people.

Young workers were also the focus of the third initiative which was again based on research that the CNV had conducted into the pay of young disabled workers, finding that they had experienced barriers to entry and to progression, leaving them more vulnerable to low pay. The union's early response was to set up a special hot-line for young disabled workers to encourage them to tell their stories and to seek justice. Importantly the union's actions led to a change in the law which is now focused on getting young disabled people into work.

The Limits of EU Law

Legislation by itself has not proved sufficient to effectively combat discrimination in employment. There are a number of reasons for this, including the fact that the European Commission has limited powers, beyond encouraging Member States to introduce measures that challenge non-discrimination. All Member States have now transposed the directives into national law, including the provisions that relate to the role of trade unions, and although the Directives indicate that these provisions are to be applied in accordance with national law and practice and in some Member States such provisions may limit the ability of the trade unions to intervene; nevertheless it is clear that the Directives recognise both the trade unions and employers as legitimate interest parties. Transposition of course has been mixed and in some cases the European Commission has instituted infringement proceedings, including against Belgium, Finland, Hungary, Italy, the Netherlands, and the UK. Criticism of the effectiveness of the legislation has been voiced both by EU level bodies and in the European-wide surveys conducted by the European Commission. A report by the European Network of Legal Experts in the Non-discrimination Field (Chopin and Uyen Do, 2012: 147) notes that while the directives have 'immensely enhanced legal protection against discrimination' 'a small number of shortcomings still appear to remain in the legislation of some Member States and candidate countries'. The experts also note that relatively few cases have been taken by individuals seeking to assert their legal rights and that there is a wide discrepancy between levels of discrimination experienced and that reported and that this is in part due to low awareness among both the public and the legal profession as to the nature of the rights there are. Eurobarometer 2012, for example, found that half of the respondents would not know their rights if they were victims of discrimination or harassment and that even for those who were identified as members of minority groups, awareness was not much higher, although awareness was heightened and influenced by age, length of education and subjective urbanisation. In 2013 the Committee on Employment and Social Affairs of the European Parliament published a draft motion to the Parliament (Kosa, 2013) which states that the legislation 'does not cover discrimination effectively' and that there is a 'lack of consistency' in the implementation of existing legislation at Member State level. AGE Platform Europe too has also raised concerns about the complexity of the jurisprudence emerging from the Court of Justice of the European Union (CJEU) which it described as 'not challenging only for legal professionals, but even more so for employers and employees who want to apply it or seek protection'. The 2012 Eurobarometer survey also reveals widespread concern about the effectiveness of the Directives to deliver non-discrimination, with one in three Europeans (31%) saying that efforts made in their country are not effective and nearly half (45%) suggesting this in relation to the Roma. Curran and Quinn looking at the impact of legislation on employment relations practice note:

> Legislation is not the primary initiator of change. In the case of race equality the market was found to be a key determinant of practice. However, regulation can influence change in organisations, depending on the complex dynamic between a number of contingencies, including the aspect of employment being regulated, the presence of supportive institutions and organisation-specific variables (2012: 464).

Social Dialogue and Equality

The study on workplace equality identified 27 social partner initiatives categorised as significant or innovative, including training agreements and, one example was an agreement signed between the Vienna City administration and the Austrian Federation of Trade Unions (GdG). A majority of the initiatives identified (20 out of the 27) had been taken at national level, suggesting that initiatives are more likely where they are the outcome of a national policy that applies generally to the whole union. By contrast, sectoral and local agreements were relatively rare. Prior to the economic crisis and the implementation of the austerity measures the Greek Athens Labour Centre (EKA) trade union and the

Hellenic Federation of Enterprises (SEV) employers' organisation had signed a collective agreement which set penalties on employers who discriminated. Other examples included that of the UK Communication Workers Union (CWU) which had, in conjunction with the employer, established Dignity at work groups. The Democratic Confederation of Free Trade Unions (LIGA) in Hungary had concluded equal opportunity plans in public administration with the relevant employers. The Irish Municipal, Public and Civil Trade Union (IMPACT) had negotiated a framework equality agreement with each of the employers it negotiated with. The Spanish General Workers' Union (UGT) had concluded an agreement with the Federation of Commerce, Hotels, and Restaurants on an agreed framework for the implementation of equality plans. In the Mapping study social dialogue was most frequently identified in relation to racial/ethnic origin and in the interviews conducted with trade union respondents it was clear that they were most likely to identify their commitment to equality in relation to the promotion of non-discrimination on this ground. In relation to ethnic origins, the Danish Timber, Industry and Construction Workers' Union (TIB) and the Danish Construction Association had an agreement on methods to encourage minority ethnic youth into the sector. The Austrian Federation of Trade Unions (OEGB), together with the Upper Austrian Economic Chamber and the Austrian Employment Service, had set up a 'Centre of competence in migration issues', to provide for the recognition of migrant worker qualifications. In Belgium, the Flemish government and the social partners had signed an agreement on raising awareness of labour market discrimination against minority ethnic workers. There were also examples of social dialogue to promote equality in relation to sexual orientation. The Dutch National Federation of Christian Trade Unions (CNV) had signed a Covenant between the Netherlands Trade Union Confederation (FNV), The Confederation of Netherlands Industry and Employers (VNO-NCW) and Federation of Dutch Trade Unions (FNV) and individual companies, which were united in the Company Pride Platform on sexual orientation under the slogan 'Equal treatment at the workplace regardless of sexual orientation', aimed at stimulating the labour market participation of LGBT peoples. The Mapping survey found many examples of social partner agreements to deliver specific changes to workers' terms and conditions to meet the requirement not to discriminate. For example, the Portuguese General Confederation of Portuguese Workers (CGTP) had negotiated an agreement with the employers in the manufacturing sector that applied to migrant cleaning workers, allowing them to accumulate two months of their holiday entitlement to travel back to their home countries. A collective agreement in the hotels sector in Brussels had been negotiated by the General Federation of Belgian Labour (FGTB) to ensure that Moroccan women workers in the sector had the same pay entitlements as local workers. The Icelandic Confederation of Labour (ASI), had reached a collective agreement with the Confederation of Icelandic Employers (SA) on the treatment of foreign workers in the labour market. The Dutch trade union FNV had negotiated collective agreements on pre-training (including language training) for prospective recruits to the police from minority ethnic communities. In relation to discrimination on the grounds of religion or belief, social dialogue had also been used to find solutions to accommodate the religious needs of workers. These measures generally were aimed at promoting working arrangements that took account of the religious needs of workers in terms of hours of work, holidays, clothing and diet. In Sweden, for example, the trade union Handels Uppsala had reached agreement with the employers that gave workers from non-majority religions time off for religious holidays. In the UK, the fire fighters' union FBU had persuaded the employer to conduct research into the issue of the use of breathing apparatus and facial hair, which finally got the employer to accept that the uniform requirements imposed on its workers, which effectively excluded some groups from applying for jobs, were to do with a corporate image rather than health and safety. Disability was another strand of discrimination where unions had successfully achieved collective agreements. In Bulgaria the Confederation of Independent Trade Unions (CITUB) had negotiated longer annual leave for disabled workers. In Iceland, the ASI trade union had negotiated a wage agreement to improve the labour market position of disabled workers. The Italian General Confederation of Labour (CGIL) had negotiated for the right of the relatives of disabled people to take paid sabbaticals of up to two years. The Polish Electric Machine Industry Trade Union (ZZPE) had taken a proactive role in combating disability discrimination, reporting to the Mapping study:

> When we entered a company, we pointed out our fields of interest and signed pacts of non-discrimination with employers. We proved that coming out on disability is beneficial for both employees and employers. People started to believe that they will not face any problems because of their disability and they will get some privileges – shorter time of work, longer holidays and special funds from social fund.

> We thought that employers do not want to employ the disabled because they are afraid of problems, but it turned out that employers just do not know anything about disabled employees and possible benefits. When we prepared local trade union activists and they knew the employment procedures and they could help employers – the whole chain started, disabled people found employment. The global crisis slowed it down but before there was a strong tendency. Employers also invested in special solutions for disabled employees – special elevators, special job positions, rooms etc. (Poland, trade union interviewee).

In relation to age, some agreements had involved the abolition of terms that disadvantaged younger workers. The Bulgarian Confederation of Labour (Podkrepa) had negotiated the abolition of a bonus system based on seniority. The Finish Trade Union of Education (OAJ) had negotiated agreements that took account of age in the management of training. The rule that pensions were based on final salary had been abolished, allowing teachers to reduce their commitment to taking additional courses in their last months of work. The German Construction, Agriculture, Environment (IGBAU) trade union had concluded a number of agreements with employers that abolished lower rates for young workers or apprentices. The Slovakian Confederation of Trade Unions (KOZ SR) has negotiated a clause in its collective agreements that placed a duty on employers not to dismiss workers within five years of retirement. Similarly the Romanian Federation of Light Industry Trade Unions (Petricontex) had negotiated a collective agreement with employers at federation level to deal with the mass job losses in cases of restructuring.

In general the trade union participants were positive about the engagement of employers in these social dialogue initiatives. However a minority indicated that while agreements might have been reached with employers it was more difficult to achieve concrete outcomes.

Conclusion

The Mapping study of course coincided with the start of the worst economic crisis in living memories. The EU economy shrank by around 4% in the two years up to the end of 2009 (European Commission, 2009) and as a consequence of downturn millions of workers lost their jobs, while many who remained in work had experienced cuts in pay, hours of work or other benefits, including pensions. Austerity measures were introduced in a number of Member States; most notably, Greece, Spain, Ireland, Portugal, Hungary and Latvia, but the ripples had spread more widely so that no countries were immune from the effect of crisis, and in every Member State collective bargaining and trade union influence had been challenged. Some of the trade unions surveyed in the Mapping study made a connection between their more limited ability to negotiate on equality issues and the crisis, as one respondent noted: 'in times of economic crisis it is very difficult to persuade managers to employ persons with disabilities'. Several trade union respondents reported similarly with regard to discrimination on the ground of ethnicity, with one respondent noting 'due to economic crisis everyone is afraid of losing his/her job and prejudices are arising and are manifested'. Trade unions also reported some employers had used the cover of the economic crisis to undermine working conditions or to refuse to implement improvements. Thus crisis both limited the ability of trade unions to combat racism, directly through a shift in focus to the protection of existing terms and conditions and to the job protection of their members and indirectly as a consequence of employer response. This is not to say that the economic crisis had caused trade unions to abandon their commitment to equality. The Mapping study found that those unions with a strong equality ethos were less likely to suggest that the crisis had forced them to put this on hold. It could indeed be argued that the economic crisis provided a cover, for both trade unions and employers, where they have a low level of commitment to combating inequality.

As we have suggested in this chapter, within the European Union discrimination and disadvantage are still prevalent. In a period of economic crisis, policies to ensure equality of treatment have been constantly challenged, as governments, employers and other social actors promoted measures that had the potential to undermine equality. As a 2012 report on the application of the EU Charter on Fundamental Rights notes:

> The year 2012 witnessed a number of serious incidents of racism and xenophobia in the EU, including racist and xenophobic hate speech and violence against Roma and immigrants. Data collected by the EU Fundamental Rights Agency indicated that, on average, minorities are victims of assault or threat more often than the majority population (European Commission, 2012: 3).

AGE Platform Europe similarly noted that while Council Directive 2000/78/EC had begun to have a:

> 'noticeable effect in combating age discrimination' prior to the start of the economic crisis 'the positive effects for older workers have diminished since the crisis began and it is apparent that a strong link exists between the economic crisis and an increased perception of age discrimination ... [and that] ... the economic crisis has brought with it a marked difference in the effectiveness with which the Employment Directive is being implemented' (2013: 2).

This is also confirmed in the 2012 Eurobarometer survey where two-thirds of respondents were reported as believing that the economic crisis had contributed to more discrimination against older people, while more than half believed that it had contributed to an increase in discrimination in the labour market on the grounds of disability and ethnic origin. There had also been a rise by five percentage points since 2009 (to 54%) of respondents reporting that due to the economic crisis, policies promoting equality and diversity were regarded as less important and that they were receiving less funding. This was particularly of concern for those Europeans with a disability, 63% of whom believed this to be the case in relation to policies countering discrimination.

Chapter 4
Types of Initiatives across Europe

The challenges posed by economic globalisation make it imperative that civil society organisations break down the barriers that have traditionally divided them, in order to ensure that the rights of those who are marginalised or vulnerable are kept firmly on the international agenda. In particular, globalisation brings fresh impetus to the need to forge alliances between the trade union movement and NGOs concerned with social and economic development. While there is plenty of evidence of successful cooperation, major problems, fears, suspicions, and at times hostilities remain between them. Some of these are substantial and sharp policy differences, but others are the consequence of colliding political or organisational cultures, prejudices, financial competition, and a mutual lack of understanding of respective roles and objectives (Spooner, 2004: 19).

This is the first of our chapters that focus specifically on the initiatives taken by trade unions on anti-discrimination. Its aim is to examine in some detail those European-wide trade union practices which were identified in the Mapping study and, in particular, those that involved trade unions engaging with Non-Governmental Organisations (NGOs). As Spooner (2004) points out in the quotation that is at the head of this chapter, there is a need to 'forge alliances' between trade unions and NGOs. In this chapter we look at these alliances through the lens of European level action. In Chapter 6 we focus more generally on the linkages between trade unions at national and local level and NGOs. Here we explore the nature of the initiatives undertaken at European level, looking at their type, duration and longer-term impact. The aim is to understand why certain initiatives were pursued, what the context was for their introduction and why some appeared to have greater resonance or have a more long-lasting impact than others. In this way we hope to prepare the ground for the thematic exploration of initiatives in the subsequent chapters. The chapter therefore begins by providing an overview of the policies, as reported to the Mapping study, by the European level trade unions. It explores what has happened in relation to each of these initiatives since the time when they were first developed. It is important to make it clear that the aim of this chapter is not to cover every policy adopted by EU level trade unions, but only those policies which were identified in the Mapping study. The reason for limiting the analysis to these alone is because it allows us to focus on policies which the unions themselves believed were significant or innovative and which they had identified as being aimed at tacking discrimination. Our overall aim is not to demonstrate that the initiatives have of themselves necessarily introduced identifiable changes but rather to posit that their adoption provided an impetus for union-led actions at confederation and national level within the Member States. Thus the initiatives cannot be assessed on the basis of their specific outcomes without taking account of their potential for influencing trade union behaviours.

Metcaff et al. (2001) have argued that trade unions have played a significant role in reducing discrimination, suggesting that dispersion in pay is lower among union members than among non-members. Foster and Fosh suggested, in relation to disability, that despite the role of NGOs in supporting those with disabilities, unions remain 'the only workplace actors who are capable of reconfiguring the personal as political and integrating disability concerns in wider organisational agendas' (2009: 560). More recently Hogue and Bacon (2014) provide a more nuanced interpretation of union-effect, demonstrating that while there is an association between union recognition and the adoption of a range of equal opportunity policies, this association is most evident where unions can influence equal opportunities' decision-making, either through negotiation or consultation. Importantly it did not appear to matter which route was taken but the absence of either reduced the trade union effect. However, all of these previous studies focused only on UK-based trade unions and furthermore did not distinguish the policies of national unions from those of the lead Confederation, in the case of the UK, the Trades Union Congress (TUC). Yet McKay, (2011) reviewing the impact of EU level legislation on trade unions, does suggest that while legislation (in the form of the EU Directives discussed in Chapter 3) was insufficient to encourage trade unions to take up issues of non-discrimination, the role of EU-level trade unions was crucial. It is this proposition that we explore more fully in this chapter.

The European Trade Union Confederation (ETUC) is the leading European trade union organisation. Established in 1973 it now comprises 85 national confederations in 36 countries, together with ten European trade union federations. It is organised on the basis of a Congress which adopts its general policy and which meets every four years. An elected Executive Committee determines the direction of the ETUC in between its congresses, while a Secretariat manages its day-to-day affairs. It describes itself as a 'pluralist' organisation, representing all workers at European level. It has a Women's Committee, a Youth Committee and a European Federation of Retired and Older People. It does not negotiate with individual employers and has no direct representation structures for any of the discrimination strands, such as LGBT, ethnicity, disability or religion or belief that are included within the non-discrimination requirements of the EU Directives. Its aims are to influence European decision making and it was in that role that it was the trade union signatory to three social partner framework agreements in the field of non-discrimination, those on parental leave,[1] part-time work[2] and fixed-term work,[3] which were incorporated into the EU directives.

The European Trade Union Committee for Education (ETUCE) is the teachers' social partner organisation at European level. It was established in 1977 and is composed of national trade unions of teachers. It is an integrated part of Education International, the worldwide teachers' body but is also a European Trade Union Federation of the ETUC. It is the social partner organisation for teachers in Europe and sees its aims as to develop and implement programmes designed to further the interests of education unions in Europe. In relation to the Mapping study the ETUCE reported the adoption of a number of initiatives which the Mapping study categorised as 'significant' or 'innovative' and it, along with the ETUC, was responsible for the seven EU level initiatives highlighted in the Mapping study. These projects are examined in subsequent sections of this chapter.

The context or background to the ETUC's work on the promotion of equality and non-discrimination was its work in relation to gender discrimination, where it has a longer history of activity, compared to that in some of the other strands, of opposing discriminatory practices. In 2005 it formally adopted a 'Framework of actions on gender equality' committing it to address gender roles, promote women in decision-making, support work-life balance measures, and tackle the gender pay gap. In 2007 the ETUC adopted a manifesto which committed it specifically to work towards the elimination of discrimination. Its more recent activities, as we suggest below, have been more focused on providing a trade union response to the effects on jobs and services of both the economic crisis and the subsequent austerity measures. With this focus it has been involved in the organisation of a number of major demonstrations across Europe. However, in relation to non-discrimination its actions have primarily been either in the production of policy or action statements or in the organisation of conferences. In some cases this has involved working with the social partner representatives from the employer side (for example on the framework agreements) but a more interesting development has been in relation to its work with NGOs which we explore more fully in Chapter 6. Here

---

1 Council Directive 2010/18/EU, of 8 March 2010, implementing the revised Framework Agreement on parental leave concluded by BUSINESSEUROPE, UEAPME, CEEP and ETUC and repealing Directive 96/34/EC.

2 Council Directive 97/81/EC of 15 December 1997 concerning the Framework Agreement on part-time work concluded by UNICE, CEEP and the ETUC – Annex: Framework agreement on part-time work.

3 Directive 1999/70/EC on the Framework Agreement on fixed-term work concluded by ETUC, UNICE and CEEP.

it had reached accords in the area of employment around specific issues, or had published joint statements. An example of this is its work with ILGA-Europe, the European region of the International Lesbian, Gay, Bisexual, Trans and Intersex Association. With ILGA-Europe, the ETUC has organised a number of activities aimed at ensuring a trade union presence in issues of LGBT rights. This was a ground-breaking direction for the ETUC to take, as it forced trade unions at national level to then review their policies and practices in relation to LGBT rights. Indeed, as a number of national trade union respondents to the Mapping study indicated, without the impetus from the ETUC they would not have pursued policies at national level. It is for these reasons that the ETUC's work with ILGA-Europe was identified, in the Mapping study, as one of the seven significant initiatives taken at EU level.

As already discussed the ETUC's most recent strategy and action plan (for the period 2011 to 2015)[4] focuses primarily on the economic crisis and on the impact of austerity measures on jobs and on job opportunities, particularly for young people, reflecting the seriousness of the problem in Europe where one in three young people is unemployed. But this focus has inevitably impacted on the extent to which a wider range of policies in relation to non-discrimination are pursued in this difficult context. Of the ten strategy objectives covered in the action plan for 2011–15, there is only one that looks specifically at equality and social cohesion and at the principles of non-discrimination. It does restate the ETUC's commitment to:

- Fight for effective equal rights for all and against all forms of sexism, racism, xenophobia, discrimination on the basis of gender, religion, age, disability, gender assignment and sexual orientation;
- Exert pressure to ensure the adoption by the European Council of the proposed directive protecting against discrimination in all areas of life; and
- Promote the exchange of good experience, while exploring the possibilities for developing guidelines or codes of conduct with employer organisations at EU level.

It also continues the ETUC's support for gender mainstreaming[5] but these are not necessarily key priority issues. The action plan did set out that a member of the ETUC Secretariat should have responsibility for gender equality and has also committed the organisation to continue with its annual survey on the gender distribution of its own decision-making structures, working towards a

---

4 http://www.etuc.org/sites/www.etuc.org/files/other/files/rapport_congres_2011_en_def_1.pdf.

5 The ETUC had adopted a Charter on gender mainstreaming in trade unions at its Seville Congress in 2007.

gender-balanced composition on its Executive Committee by 2015. However, it is obvious that the crisis has forced it to redirect its activities towards promotion of employment.

Framing Equality Initiatives at EU Level

The European level respondents to the Mapping study highlighted a number of initiatives adopted in the period since 2006, of which six were identified as significant and a seventh as innovative. Of the seven initiatives, five were campaigns where the ETUC or the ETUCE worked with a relevant NGO. One was a research-focused initiative but which again involved the unions researching with NGOs. The seventh was a project where the ETUCE worked with teachers in various member states to deliver higher quality education to children of Roma heritage, using the experience and knowledge of NGOs active in Roma issues. It is primarily these seven initiatives which are explored in this chapter. These initiatives all had some aspects in common; primarily they all involved the ETUC or the ETUCE and in every case they were working in partnership with NGOs. It was this type of collaborative work that took the initiatives beyond just abstract statements into practical efforts to involve the trade unions in working with actors that historically have not been associated with trade union organisation. Indeed the two types of organisation have traditionally operated in very different ways, as the form of organisation generally adopted by trade unions is hierarchical, based on written constitutions and with each different section of the union having clear areas of operation and responsibility. Members have constitutional rights that derive from membership and decision-making bodies mostly operate on the basis of their constitutional powers and cannot go beyond them. NGOs are more varied organisational forms. They may be long-established, they may have formal constitutions and they may have a membership base that determines their policy direction. But these are not absolute pre-requisites for the NGO to operate and even where they do, from the trade union perspective, there may be a tension between trade union structures of organisation and decision-making activities and the limits that these place on them, and the more fluid structures of NGOs. Trade unions may consider that they have a greater degree of legitimacy because they have a membership to whom they are accountable and may view the NGO as a less unaccountable body influenced by personalities or politics that are not subject to membership control or scrutiny. Braun and Gearhart (2004) also point to tensions which result 'from the inherent structural differences between interest-driven trade unions and ideals-driven human rights NGOs' and claim that these differences play themselves out:

in how these actors pursue social justice in a globalised economy. Human rights' NGOs tend to see codes of conduct as a method to prevent violations, akin to their traditional work on legal reform and human rights' monitoring. Trade unions assess codes for their potential to help empower workers, especially to help ensure freedom of association, which will lead to the realisation of participatory rights (2004: 183).

Compa (2004) recognises that there are tensions between trade unions and NGOs but also argues that they have more in common than with corporations, governments or international organisations. Thus there may be convincing reasons as to why they should work together.

The other area of commonality between the institutions identified in the Mapping study, beyond the fact that they were working with NGOs, was that most of the initiatives were reliant on European-level funding to sustain them. This may have had both positive and negative consequences, as while it might encourage trade unions to take up equality issues, where otherwise they might not, it also makes the continuation of the activities dependent on continued funding. As the Mapping study made clear, the existence of funding streams both empowers trade unions (where these enable them to take on new initiatives) but also runs the risk of unions focusing on those areas where funding is available, rather than on those where action is most needed. Thus the existence of funding potentially shapes the direction of trade union initiatives in the field of non-discrimination. Importantly, in relation to the European initiatives highlighted in the Mapping study, these had generally been transformational for both the trade unions and the NGOs, but for the former in particular. In a number of cases the core location of activity was not the workplace, and trade unions were therefore not only engaging with new actors but outside of their arena of normal activity. It is this, rather than the outcomes they may or may not have achieved, that makes the initiative's highlighted so significant.

Case study example B

The first of the seven initiatives identified in the Mapping study was the *Manifesto of the ETUC in addressing discrimination*. The ETUC highlighted this as one of its most significant actions in the fight against discrimination. In essence it amounted to a 'framing' initiative providing a road map for the general direction that European level trade unions were recommended to take to counter discrimination and to promote equality of opportunity. The *Manifesto* was adopted by the ETUC at its 11th statutory conference held in Seville in 2007. It encompassed five key areas, committing the

ETUC to 'go on the offensive' on these broad fronts: the European labour market; the promotion of social dialogue, collective bargaining and worker participation; effective European economic, social and environment governance; for a stronger Europe; and for stronger unions and a stronger ETUC. It is notable that these lofty aims were adopted just a month before the European Central Bank issued a statement expressing its concern that markets were increasingly vulnerable, and three months before the European Banking Federation noted that 'tensions related to US sub-prime mortgages' were starting 'to cause shortages of liquidity in money markets around the world'.[1] Thus the commitment by the ETUC to the promotion of non-discrimination came at exactly the time when the first flickers of crisis were emerging. The *Manifesto* states that the ETUC supports:

a Europe which is both 'more' and 'better'; a Europe which is integrated around rights and values including peace, liberty, democracy, fundamental rights, equality, sustainable development, full employment and decent work, social dialogue, the protection of minorities, universal and equal access to high quality public services, and a successful economy which supports social progress and employment protection.

The policy was described as 'a new stage' in the ETUC's development 'towards an organisation which is stronger, more cohesive and more influential in benefiting the workers or Europe and the world'. In the area of non-discrimination, the *Manifesto* committed the ETUC to:

- Prioritise the elimination of the wage gap between men and women; and
- Always promote equality and gender mainstreaming;
- Always fight racism, discrimination and xenophobia;

At the same Congress, and following the publication of the results of a questionnaire survey conducted in 2006 (ETUC, 2007) which demonstrated continuing inequalities, the ETUC also adopted a *Charter on gender mainstreaming in trade unions*. This committed it to demand 'the inclusion of gender equality among the fundamental values of the EU'. The Charter focused only on gender pay equality and other factors of gender discrimination, such as the gender representation gap. It was accompanied by a Congress Statement on minimum wages, equality and

---

1 http://www.preceden.com/timelines/30876-european-debt-crisis-timeline.

49

collective bargaining that was said to amount to 'an offensive on pay: towards equality'. The Charter did not concern itself directly with other aspects of inequality that might arise in relation to the other strands of discrimination, such as disability, sexuality or age.

By its 12th statutory conference in 2011, the ETUC's priorities had inevitably shifted at least to some extent. This was as a consequence of the wider labour market changes which the ETUC was not able to halt or reverse. Thus whereas the five broad fronts proclaimed in 2007 envisaged an expanding labour market and improvements in pay and conditions, the demands which were advanced at the 2011 Congress were more focused, concentrating on the prevention of a collapse of labour markets and aiming to secure employment and protect wages. It is instructive that the 2011 Congress was held in Athens, the geographical heart of the economic crisis, and that this in turn was the location for the presentation of a new *Manifesto*, proclaiming that 'the central issue for European trade unions at present is the financial crisis affecting Greece, Ireland and Portugal and the more general policy of austerity governance in other member states, exerting downward pressure on pay, public services, social security, pensions and labour and living standards'. By then it was apparent that some of the core issues contained in the Seville *Manifesto* would be absent from the later Athens *Manifesto*. The promotion of equality, which was the centrepiece of five broad fronts in the Seville Manifesto, in Athens was relegated to the 12th out of 20 points in the new *Manifesto*[2] stating that the ETUC would:

> Work actively for gender equality and fight against all forms of discrimination on the grounds of sex, race, religion, age, disability and sexual orientation.

---

2 The Athens Manifesto (2011) http://www.etuc.org/sites/www.etuc.org/files/other/pdf/manifest_new_en.pdf.

All of the other European level initiatives classified as significant or innovative in the Mapping study were assisted or supported by the prior existence of the *Manifesto*. Already at an Executive Committee of the ETUC held in October 2007 it was reported that the adoption of the *Manifesto* had led to a number of specific outputs. These included social partner consultation on the reconciliation of work, private and family life and in relation to gender mainstreaming and the development of leadership courses for women in trade unions. At the

Executive Committee meeting that year a statement confirmed that the *Manifesto* had 'led to the development of discrimination-specific initiatives' such as the cooperation with the NGO ILGA-Europe in jointly challenging discrimination on the grounds of sexuality or sexual preference (see below).

The second of the seven initiatives involved the ETUC working with both the European Commission and NGOs. The context is as follows. In June 2009 the European Commission held its annual anti-discrimination conference, but taking a new direction by focusing on the role of NGOs and trade unions in combating discrimination. A draft joint statement was agreed and issued in October 2009 as the Joint Declaration. *Fight discrimination and guarantee equality for all*. Importantly it was addressed to the EU as well as to the Member States and was signed by the ETUC and the Social Platform (representing European level NGOs) (European Commission, 2009). It called for:

- Adoption by the European Council of the proposed Art 13 directive protecting discrimination on the grounds of age, disability, religion or belief, and sexual orientation in all areas of life;
- The tackling of remaining gender gaps and ensure gender mainstreaming;
- Investment in strong social policies and public services that support equality;
- The development of rights-based migration and integration policies; and
- Work in strong partnership with trade unions and civil society organisations at European and national level.

Exploring European Level Initiatives on Specific Grounds

We now move on to looking at the six other specific European level initiatives in the Mapping study. These cover three of the main strands of discrimination as set out in Council Directives 2000/43/EC and 2000/78/EC, specifically discrimination on the grounds of sexual orientation, ethnicity and disability. In every case the European level trade union body worked with its NGO counterpart to undertake the initiative.

It has been in campaigning around LGBT issues that the ETUC appears to have been most proactive in relation to equality issues since the 2007 *Manifesto* and its actions here represent both the second and third of the European-level initiatives. A senior official of the ETUC, in an interview for the Mapping study, explained why in its view it was important to challenge stereotypes, even within unions, and to be seen as an organisation that defended LGBT rights:

> They give that being Lesbian or Gay is a personal matter – don't bring it into the union. That is still a deeply rooted notion that being Lesbian or Gay is about sex. It's nothing to do with sex but about how you are treated.

The ETUC's campaigning initiatives have been supported and encouraged through its close cooperation with the main EU level NGO, ILGA-Europe. The background to this new direction for the ETUC was as follows. Once the Seville *Manifesto* had been adopted the ETUC launched an '*Extending equality*' project bringing together its member organisations, in partnership with the ILGA-Europe. The aim was to develop a clearer picture of what was happening at national level in the Member State trade unions in relation to LGBT issues and also to encourage the exchange of best practice. A survey of ETUC member confederations was undertaken and presented in 2008 at a two-day conference, the first such Europe-wide trade union conference on LGBT rights. A representative of the Italian General Confederation of Labour (CGIL) described the project (in an interview during the Mapping study) as:

> Already producing its first results not only in terms of awareness-raising at EU level, but also in terms of the involvement of the local trade unions in engaging in the LGTB anti-discrimination field (Italy, trade union interviewee).

A four-year action programme addressing LGBT issues was announced in partnership with ILGA-Europe and financed by the European Commission. Its aims were for the production of awareness-raising material and for more activities to ensure that affiliates integrated support for LGBT workers into their equality work. The programme also promoted a decision taken at the 2008 conference to the effect that the ETUC should officially take part in the Euro-pride march to take place the following year in Stockholm. Showing that the trade union movement regarded LGBT issues as trade union issues and that it was willing to send senior members of its executive to the Euro-pride march was a ground-breaking action with both the ETUC President Wanja Lundby-Wedin and Confederal Secretary of the ETUC Catelene Passchier, participating in a seminar on LGBT rights and trade union rights which was organised during the Euro-pride event. The Mapping survey report noted in relation to this initiative:

> The project strengthened dialogue between the trade unions and ILGA-Europe, the NGO representing LGBT organisations at EU level. This cooperation continued around the organisation of the World-Out games. Importantly it also developed sustainable actions to be carried forward in relation to trade union policies in Europe and at national level. The impact of the initiative has been to legitimise union actions in relation to sexual orientation in a number of European countries. Without this initiative it is unlikely that all of the national-level initiatives identified in the study would have come about (2010: 15).

The initiative around the sporting and social event, the World Outgames is the next of the initiatives examined here. A resolution at the 2008 conference called on the ETUC to add its support to the organisation of the World Outgames. This social and sporting event had first been held in Montreal, Canada in 2006, following a split in the organisation of the Gay Games (Washington and McKay, 2011). Copenhagen was to be the location of the second World Outgames in 2009 and the first time they would take place in Europe. For the unions to identify with this event was an important step in bringing their activities around LGBT issues to a wider audience. It thus was one of the initiatives identified in the Mapping study as 'significant', for two reasons. First, it required close cooperation between the ETUC and ILGA-Europe and therefore represented a new direction of organisation for the ETUC. Second it required it to engage beyond its traditional areas of activity. The involvement in the World Outgames required the ETUC to campaign both for the games to be held in Europe and for a trade union presence, not in the context of collective bargaining, social dialogue or the other areas of its customary engagement. Working to promote what was essentially a sporting activity represented an important new direction.

The fourth European level initiative explored here and selected in the Mapping study was the first of those initiated by the ETUCE, the education trade union, and it addressed the education of Roma children. *Developing non-discriminatory quality education for Roma children* was a project funded by the European Commission following an application initiated by the ETUCE. The project had been proposed in response to the publication of data demonstrating a severe imbalance in the provision of education to Roma children in Central and Eastern Europe and was originally raised by the Dutch affiliated education trade union. In an interview conducted during the Mapping study, a spokesperson for the ETUCE stressed the importance of the project for the union:

> So this has been a very big step forward, it's been really important for them [teachers] to suddenly realise that we all have hidden stereotypes and prejudices in our head and even when you are teaching you are doing it without realising that it's something that you have in your way of proceeding with the children and this was a very good tool to warn them, it's something that you are doing, you don't realise that you are and this is, of course, something that it is illegal. It was a process for them [...] to be able to recognise some practices that could be discriminatory and they just didn't know.

The Roma in Europe face high levels of social exclusion, poverty, discrimination and isolation. Roma children are more likely to be in segregated institutions, receiving sub-standard education and the issue of low levels of educational achievement is acknowledged. A report by Unicef published in 2011 states that 'discrimination and non-inclusive school systems systematically deprive children from Roma communities of their right to education' (Lansdown, 2011: 2). In much of Central and Eastern Europe only one in five Roma children receive primary education and, according to Unicef, those that do enrol are more likely to drop out before the end of basic schooling, 'because of racism in schools and the ill preparation of schools to meet their needs'.

The focus of the initiative was on access to education for Roma children, particularly in Bulgaria, Slovakia and Hungary, three Member States with large Roma populations. Between 2007 and 2009 conferences, legal seminars, training seminars and workshops were organised and national action plans produced, working with education unions in each of the three countries, providing concrete ideas to address the educational deficit experienced by Roma children, particularly as a result of their exclusion from mainstream education. The project developed tools to increase the capacity of teachers to teach in multicultural classes; it directly trained 25 trainers in each of the three countries who were subsequently responsible for training in their own countries, leading to a total trained workforce of more than 700 teachers from the three target countries. Towards the end of 2013, in response to a complaint over the continuing problem of educational exclusion for the Roma, Martin Rømer, the Director of ETUCE, issued the following statement on the 2007 programme:

> Committed union representatives and teachers dedicated to their work and the improvement of the situation for Roma children's access to education took part in the project … . This ensured that the project aims and objectives were reached on schedule and in a satisfactory way.[6]

The ETUCE also stressed that barriers to implementing anti-discrimination measures included both the lack of resources and the trade union need to prioritise 'core' issues, such as job losses, particularly in the light of the economic situation. Since the end of the project it had been attempting to broaden its focus to intercultural education, but had not been successful in gaining funding for this due to change in financing for programmes in EC, with fewer open calls for proposals. The ETUCE described its experiences of working on the project as 'a very positive experience' stating that as a consequence:

> Trade unions established National Action Plans for each country, with concrete suggestions and actions on how to improve the situation of Roma children's access to quality education. The final aim of the process, initiated through this project, is to ensure that Roma children can enjoy equal access to education. An important element in this process towards equal access to education is the capacity of teachers to approach and deal with different cultures in the classroom.

---

6 Source: http://www.ei-i.e.org/en/news/news_details/2781.

During the project tools to increase teachers' capacity to teach multicultural classes were developed and 750 teachers were trained in these tools.[7]

Initiative number five was around disability issues. Again this was an initiative developed by the ETUCE and, as with the ETUC projects on LGBT issues, the union worked with the European level NGO, the European Disability Forum (EDF), in a project that involved the organisation of a conference on more and better access to employment and training for workers with disabilities and, as with the work on Roma children, that was also financed by the European Commission. A further aim was to use this initiative to then lead on to a new campaign on the issue in partnership with the EDF. Thus the aim was not just to have a one off outcome but to lead to closer working relationships between the relevant NGO and the trade union. This initial collaborative work between the union and the NGO has laid a framework for continued joint work. For example, both the ETUCE and EDF were signatories to an open letter to EU head of states and governments protesting at cuts to the Europe for Citizens programme, which encouraged partnerships between civil society networks. A joint statement from the ETUC and EDF[8] published in 2011 notes:

> The ETUC and EDF acknowledge the developments achieved in the European Union in recent years, however they underline there is still a lot to be done to make an inclusive and accessible labour market become a reality. They stand against the reduction of social budgets, job insecurity, and the rise in unemployment worsened by the economic and financial crisis that affects the most vulnerable, such as disabled people (ETUC, 2011).

It would have been expected that at least one of the initiatives at EU level, reported to the Mapping study, would be on the issue of ethnicity and racial discrimination, and indeed the sixth and final significant initiative covered in this chapter was on this ground. For the ETUC the 2008 European Year of intercultural dialogue acted as a lever to put the debate on 'multi-cultural Europe' on the trade union agenda, and to more actively take part in the debate at national and European level on the 'integration' of migrants and ethnic and religious minorities. This led it to organise, with its affiliates, a trade union campaign to address all forms of racism and xenophobia, focussing on common interests and understanding ('towards unity in diversity'), to address and overcome the increasing and potentially dangerous gap between 'insiders' and 'outsiders'. The aim was to encourage joint actions at workplace and sectoral

---

7 Source: http://etuce.homestead.com/ETUCE_ROMA.html.

8 ETUC (2011) *Trade unions and the disability movement: together for a more inclusive labour market*, Brussels 14 March 2011.

level, on combating racism and xenophobia at work. The European level NGO the European Network Against Racism (ENAR) worked with the ETUC on these issues, however its cooperation was on the basis of an involvement in specific projects rather than a regular or ongoing action. However, as with many of the initiatives discussed here, the onslaught of the economic crisis meant that the potential for social partner dialogue on such issues has been much diminished.

Conclusion

In discussing the initiatives highlighted above it is important to stress that these were actions identified by the trade union bodies themselves as among their most significant or innovative. In their view, at the time of our research, these were initiatives likely to have long-term impacts, changing union policies and also influencing social dialogue. However, within months of their having been initiated the economic crisis had already begun to change the direction that the equality policy had been heading in and European level trade unions found that they had to redirect their focus away from trying to improve working conditions for their members to trying to prevent their deterioration in the face of an onslaught by the governments, employers and of course the 'Troika'.[9] This is not however to assess the initiatives as inconsequent or insubstantial. Their real contribution has been to improve the long-term relationships between trade unions and NGOs and to give the trade unions the experience of successfully working with organisations whose structures and practices might differ but whose overall objectives are often complementary. There should also be a word of caution as it must be acknowledged that the initiatives identified were all reliant on external funding, mainly from the European Union. This has two consequences: funding inevitably directs the policies of trade unions and NGOs since the requirements of funders had often determined exactly the subjects of intervention. Second, where funds were not available, or no longer available, initiatives often were not sustainable in the long term and might abruptly end, simply because the available resources had been consumed.

---

9 Comprised of the European Union, the International Monetary Fund and the European Central Bank.

Chapter 5
Trade Union Cooperation beyond National Borders

[Trade union alliances] are not produced in a vacuum but often result from social processes generated by European trade union initiatives aimed at coordinating workplace union interests while articulating those interests with the centre (Pulignano, 2005: 408).

As worker mobility in Europe has intensified in the last decade and as companies have spread out from their original national bases to set up in new locations, there has been a considerable body of research on trans-national cooperation between trade unions within the EU and a number of recent studies of this relatively new phenomenon are referenced in this chapter (for example, Gold and Rees, 2013; Larsson, 2012; Pulignano, 2005; Waddington and Hoffmann, 2000). However here we take a different starting point, as although the focus of the chapter is on trans-national cooperation, our area of examination – the strands of discrimination that were the object of the Mapping study – does not permit us to commence from the point of view of structure. Council Directive 2000/43/EC of 29 June 2000 on implementing the principle of equal treatment between persons irrespective of racial or ethnic origin and Council Directive 2000/78/EC of 27 November 2000 establishing a general framework for equal treatment in employment and occupation did not make provision for the establishment of any formal institutional structure wherein trade unions might meet to exchange information or organise solidarity in the area of non-discrimination; nor did the Directives place any obligations on employers to encourage such trans-national dialogue. Thus while the studies referred to above took, as their starting point, the pre-existence of formal structures that set out the modus of cooperation between trade unions, we cannot take this route. However, this has not meant that we have been unable to investigate trans-national initiatives in the area of non-discrimination. Indeed our examination leads us to posit that while formal structures, such as European Works Councils (EWCs) have, without doubt, served as a catalyst to exchanges of information and more cooperative forms of working between Europe's trade unions, they are not the only avenue to this end. Cooperation can arise even in the absence of a structure such as an EWC that brings trade union representatives together and it is therefore useful to also reflect on other mechanisms that might foster trans-national activities between trade unions, given that the formal structures that currently exist are unlikely to expand or be added to in a period where the economies of Europe continue to be in crisis, leading, more likely, to the breaking up of existing institutional structures, rather than to their growth, and in a context where the European Commission has no proposals for new forms of trans-national representative structures within the EU. It has been their absence that has made us look at the specific impact of other forms of regulatory change, such as the Directives of 2000, that neither require or specifically encourage collaboration on the basis of the establishment of formal structure, but as we have found, in practice can result in such exchanges. In this context, and focusing on the two non-discrimination directives, we would suggest that not only do they have a potential to encourage cooperation but have actually done so. Furthermore, such cooperation is not constrained by the rules that apply where there are formal structures and constitutions, such as in the case of EWCs, and may consequently have wider impact and go beyond those narrow spheres of influence established with respect to such bodies. The chapter begins by looking at some of the literature on trans-national cooperation, mainly drawing on studies on EWCS, as bodies which have encouraged cooperation between trade union representatives in different Member States. It then moves to look specifically at the evidence garnered in the course of the Mapping study, which suggests that the anti-discrimination Directives have provided a platform for the exchange of information by trade unions across Member States, leading to the adoption of new strategies to combat discriminatory practices. We look at how unions have developed programmes around equality issues; how they have taken account of the need to engage both with trade unions in neighbouring Member States and also with sending and receiving migration countries; and at how, in a few cases, they have been able to utilise secondments of union officials from one Member State to another, leading both to the development of common projects and to the adoption of new ways of organising. Finally, we also explore the contexts in which these collaborations have occurred, to consider whether they provide a model for further cross-border cooperation, beyond equality to embrace other workplace issues. We identify seven main drivers for cooperation between trade unions in Member States in relation specifically to non-discrimination. These are where:

- Member States share common borders;
- Pre-existing EWCs have operated as models of engagement;
- There is trans-national cooperation between labour sending and labour receiving states;
- There is involvement of EU level institutions;
- There is access to EU level funds;
- There are trade union policies specifically in relation to working with developing countries; and
- There is collaboration between trade unions and NGOs.

Chun, looking at new forms of union organisation in the USA and in South Korea, argues:

> Unions have not been derailed by the barriers to unionism presented by weakened forms of associational and structural power. Rather, they have developed new approaches for shifting the balance of power between workers, subcontracting companies and building owners based on symbolic struggles, rather than economic power or legal arguments (2013: 118).

In this way, according to Chun, unions have been required to consider new methods of organising and new rallying calls and have used moral rather than legal arguments, waged battles publicly and drawn on a range of materials to strengthen their moral authority. Exchanges of experience and an openness to learn from other initiatives is a crucial aspect of this new framework of organisation for trade unions in the 21st century. Similarly, Waddington and Hoffman (2000) argue that for unions to gain control over forms of work within the global economy, they need to integrate both at national and international level and that, particularly at European level, they have to incorporate new learning experiences through mutual exchanges. However, there are also a number of factors that might impede such cooperation, in particular differences in national systems of industrial relations and lack of intercultural competence. Larsson, in a survey on such forms of cooperation, suggests that:

> In many respects, cooperation between trade unions in Europe is well developed. This cooperation includes a variety of activities, such as exchanging information; collaborating on training programs; co-producing collective statements or agreements; participating in union actions such as signing petitions, mobilising demonstrations or organising strikes; coordinating bargaining through coordination standards or principles; coordinating negotiations on plant restructuring and closure; and negotiating with European employer organisations at sectoral and cross-sectoral levels (2012: 152).

Larsson found that cooperation was more evident in relation to soft issues, such as training, gender equality, health and safety and corporate social responsibility. For hard issues, such as collective bargaining, cooperation proved less effective. Larsson places gender and equality within his range of soft issues but does not specify further whether his reference is only to gender or to other potential strands of discrimination. For this study we have adopted Larsson's notion of 'hard' and 'soft' issues within the context of the strands of discrimination and suggest that the equality directives themselves, encompass both 'soft' issues (such as gender equality, age and disability) and 'hard' issues (such as sexual orientation, racial/ethnic origin and religion)[1] but that what the Directives have achieved in some cases, mainly through the mechanism of trans-national activity, is to encourage trade unions to move from soft to hard issues. Account of course needs to be taken of geography, history and the extent of the role given to trade unions, when considering whether there is scope for a movement from soft to harder issues. For example, Larsson et al. (2012), in a study of Nordic trade unions, found relatively high levels of cooperation with the most regular form of communication involving the exchange of information. Although there were noted differences between countries, in most cases at least half of all respondents reported this form of cooperation. Thus trade unions that already identify themselves within a particular political or geographical sphere may be more open to cooperation within that sphere of operation, although it may, at the same time, make them less open to other cooperation. The Mapping study also found that the Nordic countries tended to report initiatives based around that unit of geographical identity but were less likely to cooperate with unions in the South and in the East and West of the EU. Thus, for example, the Danish Union of Public Employees (FOA) stated that it had close Nordic cooperation in its work on supporting gay rights but did not refer to cooperation initiatives with unions beyond the Nordic states. Bernaciak (2010) found that in relation to East/West relations, that in those cases where there was an absence of local negotiation channels, Polish trade unions had gained more from the assistance of their Western counterparts (in this case German trade unionists) than from local solutions. Thus weak organisation in one country can be counteracted by strong support from another.

Forms of cross-border collaboration (where trade unions in two Member States shared a common border) were also the basis of some of the initiatives identified through the Mapping study. The Austrian Federation of Trade Unions, for example, had launched a project '*Future in the border region*' which was part financed by the European Union and part by the Federal Ministry Labour and Social Affairs, with the aim of encouraging cooperation between Austrian and Hungarian trade unions. Such initiatives were primarily aimed at ensuring that workers who lived in Hungary but worked in Austria (cross-border workers) would have the same terms and conditions as workers resident in Austria. The arrangements allowed the unions in both countries to collaborate over the flow of information to cross-border workers as well as on the production of a manual for trainers on diversity. The health sector union in the Czech Republic

---

1 We distinguish as 'soft' those issues where there is relatively widespread membership support for trade union involvement in the issue the context of a supportive public climate, so that trade unions are working within an already accepted area of intervention. 'Hard' issues are those where there is more likely to be membership antagonism or a lack of support, fostered by a public climate which is less supportive.

similarly reported well-established trans-border cooperation with unions in Germany, Poland, Austria and Slovakia.

Anner et al. (2006) suggest that international codes of conduct and framework agreements, together with the existence of EWCs or World Works Councils, enhanced union cooperation and that they provided a regulatory institutional basis for cross-border exchanges. Gold and Rees (2013) recognise the significance of directives and legislation as driving forces for trade union cooperation and actions, although again focusing on EWCs. Similarly Flynn et al. found that union responses could 'be shaped and constrained by institutional frameworks and practice, and tempered by societal expectations formed beyond the workplace' (2013: 59). Pulignano (2005), in her study of EWCs explored the extent to which cross-national union representatives' cooperation could be achieved within the context of European integration, suggesting that the extent to which Europeanisation was articulated was dependent on the voluntary context in which the EWC had been established and the orientations of the national unions towards common policy issues. Thus there are different modes of collaboration that reflect particular national experiences. In deregulated labour market contexts, such as the UK, national union affiliations to European federations, and the extent to which they played an active role therein were relevant to this involvement whereas Pulignano argues that in more regulated labour markets, the exchange of information was the motivator for cooperation, such that:

> co-ordination through the information exchange process within EWCs may become a potential (although not automatic) catalyst for the creation of alliances among employee representatives, on which cross-national trade union co-operation may be systematically constructed (2005: 407).

Martinez Lucio and Westson (2000) similarly identified flows of information within EWCs as the basis for European trade union cooperation, while Lecher et al. (2001) located cross-border networking as having the potential to contribute to European integration. Thus Puliglnano argues that relations between unions result 'from social processes generated by European trade union initiatives aimed at co-ordinating workplace union interests while articulating those interests with the centre' (2005: 408). Similarly we have found that the regulatory institutional basis represented in Council Directives 2000/43/EC and 2000/78/EC has encouraged not just the taking of initiatives within the national state, as we have demonstrated in Chapter 6, but specifically the adoption of initiatives that went beyond a single national state. EWCs provided (in some cases) models from which unions might draw comparisons in the construction of their relationships beyond their own borders. For example, in one initiative identified in the Mapping study, trade unions in Austria and

Hungary, even without the existence of an EWC, had organised to bring workers' councils with a common employer together, to deepen cooperation and to subvert company strategies that might otherwise try to play one works council off against the other.

Thirty-three national trade union respondents in the Mapping study made specific reference to trans-national or cross-border cooperation. By strand of discrimination, the largest number of references was in relation to ethnicity initiatives, representing 14 of the 33 references. Cooperation on the grounds of LGBT issues was the second most referenced, with seven of the 33 reporting cooperation initiatives on this strand. Disability and age were less likely to be as the result of trans-national cooperation, as Table 5.1 demonstrates.

Thus, as suggested above, cooperation appears able to deal with hard as well as soft issues and may indeed prioritise the former over the latter. In particular, the fact that seven initiatives on sexual orientation were directly attributable to trans-national cooperation suggests that trade unions may find strength in numbers in dealing with hard issues such as these, which may be need to be advanced even in the context of less demonstrable membership support, on the basis that they can rely on cooperation and where they can use the experiences of their colleagues in other countries to advance their programmes, particularly when dealing with a membership that may well hold homophobic opinions or have other positions which challenge Europe's equality agenda.

In addition to the cross-border initiatives referred to above there were also some examples of trans-national initiatives taken by trade unions in countries that were either sending or receiving migration. These were aimed at ensuring the protection of both host and migrant workers in the receiving states. They would involve collaboration between the key union in the sending country and the relevant union in the receiving country and were aimed at providing rights' information in the languages of the migrant workers. But they might also be used to ensure that collective bargaining rights applied. The Bulgarian Confederation of Labour, Podkrepa, highlighted one initiative to the Mapping

Table 5.1   Number of unions reporting trans-national initiatives (by strand)

Ethnicity – race	14
Sexual orientation	7
Age – young	5
Disability	4
Age – old	2
Religion – belief	1

study, on collaboration agreements with trade unions in receiving countries and reported that it had signed formal cooperation agreements with trade unions in the UK and in Spain. The General Confederation of the Portuguese Workers (CGTP) similarly reported close relationships with trade unions in countries where Portuguese workers had migrated to, with a representative in the Mapping study stating:

> We have a strategy to fight for equal conditions also in those countries. We have protocols of cooperation, bilateral cooperation, for instance with British trade unions, taking into consideration around 500,000 Portuguese that work in the UK. We have a protocol of bilateral cooperation in Luxembourg. The Portuguese who live there represent 15 per cent of the total Luxembourg population (Portugal, trade union interviewee).

In this way it can be argued that trade unions were moving beyond their traditional role in the protection of members in work in their country of origin, to promote a wider duty to protect those who migrate to other countries in search of work. Again it was through trans-national collaboration that this policy could be achieved.

The Role of European Institutions and European Funding

In a study on NGOs (in which definition they include trade unions), Cisar and Vrablikova (2013) found that the most significant indicator of cooperation was the existence of an office at EU level and membership of a trans-national network or an umbrella organisation and that 'it is organizational connectedness that contributes to lobbying' (2013: 156). Reflecting on this we have also noted that in relation to those initiatives identified in the Mapping study which had gone beyond the single Member State, European level support was a crucial component of most union cooperation, with the Mapping study final report noting:

> European-level trade union organisations played a significant role in challenging discrimination and in encouraging affiliated trade unions to take up newer issues of discrimination or issues previously not identified as trade union issues (*Trade union practices on anti-discrimination and diversity*, 2010: 14).

In Chapter 4 we looked at the initiatives classified by the survey as 'significant' that had been instigated by the European-level trade union body, the ETUC. Three were in relation to racial/ethnic origin, three on sexual orientation and one on disability, again demonstrating that 'hard' issues had dominated over 'soft' issues. Turning to look at the national trade union bodies, what emerges from the study is that the initiatives taken by the ETUC had been an important catalyst to actions at national level. Our analysis of the trade union interviews shows that out of the 187 interviews with national trade unions, 32 made reference to the ETUC. In most cases there was a single reference to their collaboration with the ETUC but in 10 cases there were two or more references. The Confederation of Independent Trade Unions in Bulgaria (CITUB) reported that it had been working with the ETUC on issues of non-discrimination. The Confederation of Labour, Podkrepa, also in Bulgaria, had worked only with ETUC but mainly through research projects and through these projects had established contact with unions in other EU countries. Most of the national union bodies referred to their working relationships with the ETUC, either in attending conferences or participating in projects. The Irish trade union confederation ICTU provided another example of an ETUC funded project, *Workplace Europe*, which had focused on trans-national cooperation on migration, while the year before it had cooperated on the ETUC project on LGBT discrimination. Another example was provided by the Netherlands Trade Union Confederation (FNV), which had cooperated with other youth departments in trade unions across Europe, with the aim of improving the situation for young workers. Similarly in the UK, the Trade Union Congress (TUC) reported that, having won equality rights for LGBT workers under UK law, it had then turned its attention to European work and had begun to work with the ETUC towards its four-year action plan *Extending equality*. As a result European trade unions began participating in annual Euro-pride demonstrations and an 11 point plan of actions had been developed.

Looking more widely at all of the initiatives reported to the survey (280 in all), a number of cases these involved a trade union or unions in one Member State working in cooperation with trade unions in one or more other Member States, in circumstances where there was access to support from EU bodies, either in the form of structural or of financial support. For example, of the 17 initiatives in relation to ethnicity identified in the survey, seven were dependent on European Union support in the form of project funding. The initiative between the Austrian and Hungarian trade unions already referred to was at least part dependent on European Union support, through a project funded by the EU. A project on flexicurity, established between trade unions in the Netherlands and in the Czech Republic, had also been financed in this way. Both the EU funding under EQUAL and PROGRESS had provided the opportunity for trade union cooperation across borders. The Greek Federation of Secondary Education School Teachers (OLME) reported that its participation in an EQUAL programme enabled the production of a series of guide books against discrimination. The Association of Free Trade Unions of Slovenia (ZSSS) referenced a European funded project targeting increasing awareness on discrimination on LGBT grounds, while the Confederation of the Independent Trade Unions in Bulgaria (CITUB) gave an example, in relation to disability discrimination, where the union stated that it had learnt a lot from the experiences of unions in other countries, particularly through its involvement in projects.

Case study example C

This example draws on data from the Italian trade union confederation, the CGIL. It was the basis for one of the Mapping case studies and highlights a number of initiatives addressing non-discrimination which have been taken by the union. The background to a range of initiatives taken by the CGIL was the establishment of an Expanded Committee on Diversity which was the outcome of a national collective agreement. The Committee was established in companies with more than 50 workers and was composed of workplace representatives, who often themselves were members of disadvantaged groups, who met annually to discuss how best to defeat discrimination. As a result of these exchanges of information, the CGIL has seen the number of claims it has taken to tribunals on behalf of its members grow substantially. One activity reported under this initiative was the establishment of a new procedure that would enable workers to compare their career progression with that of a comparable worker, in all attributes other than not being a member of a discriminated against group. Participation in EU level funded projects through EQUAL had also allowed the union to carry out training with its members in combating stereotypes. Importantly, in working with employers in large multinational companies it also led to work between it and the French trade union confederation the CGT. Thus collaboration had led to changes both within the system of national working, but also in its collaboration with organisations in other countries.

What have been the results? The CGIL reported that the work that they had done had led to the creation of groups whose focus would be on challenging discrimination. It had also contributed to the signing of a collective agreement between the two unions, other union partners and a large temporary work agency, operating in both Italy and France. It has, according to the union, contributed to better social partner dialogue. And finally its use of a panel method, for comparing and establishing discrimination, had resulted in a much clearer and well understood procedure that in turn had resulted in higher levels of compensation awards.

Sectoral Influences on Trans-national Cooperation

Trans-national cooperation may also be a reflection of policies and practices from particular sectors of employment (Marginson, 2000; Rivest, 1996). Larsson et al. found that there were sectoral differences with regard to the extent of trans-national cooperation, and that those unions that were most internationally exposed, such as in manufacturing and construction 'are more engaged in trans-national cooperation than unions in the more sheltered industries in services and professional/academic work' (2012: 40). The Mapping study also identified some initiatives that were both trans-national and sector specific. However, in contrast to Larsson et al. (2012), these were all based in the education sector. Thus while manufacturing may be found to yield a greater number of examples of trans-national cooperation, when it comes to looking specifically at anti-discrimination measures then manufacturing does not deliver the same level of trans-national initiatives.

What Could Collaboration Bring?

Based on the Mapping study findings we argue that collaboration initiatives may have the potential to extend union bargaining, negotiating and campaigning agendas in a number of new directions, although it should be stressed that this is not a given and that even the adoption of a significant initiative may lead to limited changes where there is insufficient support for it. However that is not the main subject of consideration in this chapter. We are not aiming to show that trans-national initiatives lead necessarily to successful and sustainable outcomes but rather that collaboration encourages initiatives would never come to fruition in its absence. Collaboration provides trade unions with the opportunity to build windows and links to the outside and in particular appears to allow them to go beyond soft issues to tackle hard issues. Whether or not they use these to go beyond what they define as their immediate interests, is dependent on their history, on the forces campaigning for change, on the forces resisting change and on the legal and regulatory environments in which they are operating. Collaboration also provides an environment in which unions have the opportunity to learn and to adapt their policies, practices and structures in relation to the knowledge they gain of others. One example, taken from the case studies undertaken for the Mapping study can be used to illustrate this. The All-Poland Alliance of Trade Unions (OPZZ) reported that it had established the post of national LGBT officer. This on the face appears a very radical step in a country where LGBT people are still subjected to high levels of discrimination and where the state is not particularly open to defend LGBT rights; and where a union official interviewed for the Mapping study described it as a 'taboo topic' where 'members and the officials think that it is not a trade union issue'. How this structural change came about was as a consequence of a combination of both events in Poland and of experiences gained externally. In Poland the election of a new right-wing government in 2005 found a senior government minister articulating a strongly homophobic position against gay teachers and calling for their dismissal. This had pushed the teachers' union ZNP into taking a position on LGBT issues. It joined with an LGBT NGO and eventually adopted a new trade union strategy on promoting equality. This opening up of trade unions to LGBT issues was to be the first step in a more profound change within the larger OPZZ union, but it should be stressed that without the first steps it is unlikely the structural changes it introduced would have come into being. These themselves were the result of collaboration between OPZZ and the UK trade union UNISON. OPZZ had been invited to place one of its union officials within UNISON so that the latter could benefit from the support of a Polish trade union official, in its attempts to recruit newly arriving Polish workers. The placement thus was not concerned in itself with LGBT issues. However, UNISON already had a well-established model of self-organisation for its LGBT members and had some years earlier appointed an LGBT officer with responsibility for this group of members. The OPZZ officer was committed to working on LGBT issues and noted and reported back to his union in Poland on the structure which UNISON had adopted and which appeared to give its LGBT members a stronger voice in union policies. It was proposed that a similar structure be adopted for OPZZ in Poland. This represented a completely new direction for trade unions in Poland and has without doubt contributed to more awareness of LGBT issues within the union movement. However, in the interviews which were conducted with union officials in Poland it was clear that the structural change of itself could not fundamentally change views within the union and that there was still a long way to go before it could be asserted that the policies adopted had led to real changes. For example, in the case of ZNP, a trade union official interviewed admitted that when the government minister had called for the dismissal of LGBT teachers 'almost none of union's members protested that their homosexual colleagues might be sacked'. One official from another Polish union, the Independent and Self-Governing Trade Union Solidarność (NSZZ) responded to the Mapping study: 'We will never be radical feminists or radical sexual minorities, we will help if there will be a problem, but we cannot let those groups use the union to reach their radical goals' while another official stated that while officially the union would claim to support LGBT people, in practice they were more likely to turn to OPZZ, given that NSZZ's policies were closely tied to those of the Catholic Church and thus, in her view, to anti-LGBT rights. Similarly, an official of the Trade Unions Forum (FZZ) said that he had heard of problems involving LGBT issues, but none had been addressed to the union. Thus we can demonstrate a gap between initiatives and outcomes but as we have stressed it is the initiative itself that is the focus in this chapter. Furthermore, although most of the trans-national initiatives identified in the study involved exchanges within EU Member States, a minority involved trade unions in countries beyond the EU. In all eight of the 130 initiatives identified in the study involved trade unions in Member States collaborating with unions in countries beyond the European Union, including in Zimbabwe, Russia and Brazil and these are examined further in Chapter 6. Collaboration could also take the form of attendance at international conferences that focused on non-discrimination, such as the 'Workers out' 2nd World Conference on Lesbian and Gay trade unions, held in Sidney, Australia, to which the Italian trade union CGIL reported that it had sent delegates.

Conclusion

What we have sought to demonstrate in this chapter is that there is the possibility of collaborative initiatives across and beyond Member States that confirm that trade unions do not need to only see their areas of engagement as being within national and work-related confines but that they are capable of going beyond these to take up issues that appear not to be immediately relevant to their spheres of interest. We have used the concept of 'soft' and 'hard' issues to demonstrate how cooperation between trade unions in different countries has encouraged them to adopt policies around 'hard' issues, so that collaboration not only has brought tangible results but has encouraged trade unions to challenge some of their own stereotypes or those held by their members. In particular the collaboration of national trade unions with EU level organisations has encouraged them to move from the narrow confines of restricted collective bargaining agendas to explore ways of challenging discrimination both at work and in wider society.

Chapter 6
Cooperation with Non-Governmental Organisations (NGOs) and Equality Bodies

... [the] social agenda of the labour movement could be advanced only through the building of broad popular coalitions, with the trade union movement at their centre, but bringing together many civic groups, issue-oriented movements and other popular groups that perceive, each in its own way, the social threat that corporate power represents and whose areas of concern overlap, in different degrees, with that of the labour movement (Gallin, 2000: 1).[1]

This chapter explores the relationships between trade unions and Non-governmental organisations (NGOs) in Europe: both are civil organisations whose main agendas and strategies are the improvement of society and the wellbeing of people, by acting to represent the interests and improve conditions for workers, in the case of the former and to improve mainly living conditions in the case of the latter. Gallin (2000) above suggests such trade union collaborations with other civic groups can contribute to more effective ways of fighting discrimination. As EU membership grew and its economy has become increasingly globalised, the presence of NGOs and trade unions is considered as making a dynamic contribution to civil society and the democratic process on both European and international levels. The European Commission's White Paper acknowledges this and states:

civil society plays an important role in giving voice to the concerns of citizens and delivering services that meet people's needs ... non-governmental organisations play an important role at global level in development policy. They often act as an early warning system for the direction of political debate. Trade unions and employers' organisations have a particular role and influence. The EC Treaty requires the Commission to consult management and labour in preparing proposals, in particular in the social policy field. Under certain conditions, they can reach binding agreements that are subsequently turned into Community law (within the social dialogue) (European Commission, White Paper 2001: 14–15).

---

1 Citing: Gallin, D (1980) 'Unions and transnationals: The beginnings of an international response', in *The New International Review*, Vol. 3, No. 1, New York, 1980.

According to Marschall (2002), former director of Transparency International for Central and Eastern Europe, civil society organisations are very important in achieving results when governments are not able to: 'we need civil society organizations not because they represent the people; we need them because through them we can get things done better' (Marschall, 2002: 3). There has been research that provides evidence for NGOs' successes in areas where governments have failed, for example, Hudock (1999) or Hopgood (2006). Yet their efforts are not without challenges even in cases when NGOs run successful campaigns on specific issues that gain the public's support, for example their work on an EU-wide ban on the testing of animals for the cosmetics industry, the legitimacy of activists to speak for the public is often questioned (Lang, 2012). As the quote at the start of the chapter suggests, we argue that trade union cooperation with NGOs and equality bodies, as civil society actors, has helped trade unions to broaden their equality agendas and that in some cases it has also promoted social dialogue, leading to some improvements in working conditions.

Background to NGOs

NGOs, such as religious groups, have existed in various forms for centuries, however they gained importance globally during the 1980s and 1990s, when their numbers increased rapidly and assumed a more prominent role in the area of development (Lewis and Kanji, 2009; Charnovitz, 1997). It has been estimated that there are around half a million registered NGOs worldwide and United Nations data in 2000 shows that there were around 35,000 large and established NGOs (Lewis and Kanji, 2009). According to Charnovitz (1997) four main influences accelerated the emergence of NGOs at international level: first the rise of globalisation and the integration of the world economy which led to increased intergovernmental negotiation on domestic policy; second the end of the Cold War and the period of less polarised world politics; third, the role of worldwide media – and we may now add the role of social media – which has given NGOs the opportunity of publicising their views more widely; and finally the emphasis on democratic values which raised expectations on transparency and public participation in the decision making process.

Since the 1980s NGOs have increased their profiles at local, national and international levels as they came to be recognised for their efforts in various causes, for example environmental efforts (Greenpeace), human rights (Amnesty International)[2] or their combined efforts to help victims of the tsunami in 2004 in Indonesia, India, Thailand and Sri Lanka, calling for reforms to aid systems and high profile campaigning to 'Make Poverty History'.

---

2 However both Greenpeace and Amnesty International were founded in the 1960s.

There is no single definition for NGOs. The term 'NGO' was first used in 1945 by the United Nations to distinguish between the participation of intergovernmental agencies and the non-government groups (Lang, 2012). According to the UN, partnership between the UN and NGOs has been taking place since 1947 and in accordance with Article 71 of the UN Charter, NGOs can have consultative status with the United Nations Economic and Social Council (ECOSOC). The UN definition for NGOs states:

> A non-governmental organization (NGO, also often referred to as 'civil society organization' or CSO) is a not-for-profit group, principally independent from government, which is organized on a local, national or international level, to address issues in support of the public good. Task-oriented and made up of people with a common interest, NGOs perform a variety of services and humanitarian functions, bring public concerns to governments, monitor policy and programme implementation, and encourage participation of civil society stakeholders at the community level. Some are organized around specific issues, such as human rights.[3]

According to Willetts (2002) this definition itself is quite wide, as it includes all private non-profit bodies that are not seeking public office and are not criminal organisations.

At European level NGOs are defined similarly and the term covers non-state organisations that are non-profit and work in areas for the public good, especially for protecting and promoting fundamental rights. This function distinguishes them from other organisations such as trade unions or employer associations, whose prime aim is to look after their members, although arguably trade union work has been considered as progressive as it promotes the advancement of society as a whole and not only the interests of their members. Bratton (1989) was one of the first to argue the political nature rather than economic one for NGOs, claiming that NGOs are significant supporters of civil society due to their participatory and democratic approach and Diamond (1994: 5) has called them 'a crucial source of democratic change'. Mercer (2005: 9) mentions three main arguments put forward for the role of NGOs in strengthening civil society: first, their existence as independent actors ensures plurality and opportunities for more interest groups to have a voice; second the role of NGOs in supporting marginalised groups, as NGOs tend to work with grassroots organisations or directly with communities and that often allows for greater citizen participation; and third, NGOs can check and challenge state's autonomy locally and nationally and press for change, while developing an alternative set of perspectives. Examples are given on the NGOs role in Latin American countries, especially Chile and Brazil.

---

3 For more information see http://www.unrol.org/article.aspx?article_id=23 (accessed in May 2014).

NGOs can vary in size, importance and the role they play in different societies. For this reason they constitute a complex analytical category. This plurality creates difficulties in conceptualising, defining and categorising NGOs, as highlighted in the relevant literature (Vakil, 1997; Lewis, 2010). Some are large international organisations and some are local; they carry different statuses, as some are formal and some are informal, some are bureaucratic and some are more flexible; funding can come from governments or from other organisations – in some cases even from the World Bank, while others choose different routes, such as member funding and appeals (Lewis and Kanji, 2009). This can constitute a wide gap between them as the more affluent NGOs are well-resourced and able to employ paid professional staff, while others are weaker and mainly rely on the work and financial support of volunteers. A difference is mentioned in the literature between NGOs and Grassroots Organizations (GROs) which are usually smaller organisations, often membership based and operating without paid staff and have to rely on donations or support from NGOs (Mercer, 2002). Although the distinction between the two categories is an important one, both for methodological and analytical purposes, here we will not place too much emphasis on this aspect as both NGOs and GROs can form effective partnerships with trade unions and can provide invaluable support to them to reach communities that are isolated by culture, language or physical location. For example in the Mapping study, one trade union interviewee from the Athens Labour Centre (EKA) mentioned a recent alliance between his union and a local NGO/GRO group that works with Roma communities:

> this alliance is very important to us because we are now able to approach Roma communities, discuss their needs and try to offer support. It was difficult to approach them before without the help of the group; they were suspicious of people and organisations outside their community so we were unable to gain an accurate picture of what are the main problems (Greece, trade union interviewee).

These links have been created through partnerships in previous projects such as EQUAL, through cases of common interest or through other networking events such as seminars, workshops or one-day events (Paraskevopoulou, 2010).

In terms of types of activity, NGOs in general tend to be best known for undertaking one or two main forms: the delivery of basic services to people in need, and organising policy advocacy and public campaigns for change. At the same time, NGOs have also become active in a wide range of other more specialised roles such as emergency response, democracy building, conflict resolution, human rights' work, cultural preservation, environmental activism, policy analysis, and research and information provision (Lewis and Kanji, 2009: 1). Some see NGOs in a positive light, as leading global institutes that contribute to democratic procedures in a revolutionary way (Salamon, 1993). Others are more sceptical and perceive them as unaccountable (*The Economist*, 20 September 2003) or as 'wild cards' (DeMars, 2005), or as main agencies of new 'sub-politics' (Beck, 2007). Clark (1998) questions the positive role of NGOs in the process of democratisation, especially in relation to the type of funding received by them. Scepticism also relates to the different ways NGOs function, as for example they have different motivations, beliefs and values; some are faith based organisations, while others are secular; some have charity as a core value, while others seek to empower vulnerable people. Some NGOs are structured in such a way to be ready and provide immediate humanitarian assistance and others develop longer term strategies to tackle major problems.

Salamon and Anheier (1992: 134–135) surveying the existing literature distinguished five key elements in the existing definitions of NGOs: legal (according to the legal status defined by a country), formal (registration and status), or economic/financial (in terms of the source of their income) or functional (in terms of their activity), or structural/operational (according to their basic structure and operation). Using these elements the two authors propose instead a definition that consists of the following components where the NGO:

- is formal: the organisation has 'an institutional reality' such as to be a legal entity; it has a set of formal rules and regulations or procedures; it holds formal meetings and there is a sense of organisational permanence;
- is private: the organisation is separate from the government and is not governed by governmental officials although it can be the recipient of governmental support and governmental officials can sit on its boards. However the organisation has to remain a private institution;
- is non-profit: although the organisation may accumulate some profit, this needs to go back to the organisation in order to support its mission rather than being distributed to members of its governing board (as with a private business organisation);
- is self-governing: the organisation controls its affairs and activities according to its internal procedures;
- is voluntary: the organisation is supported in its activities and management by volunteers, even if it uses professional paid staff.

Drawing on the above five characteristics, Vakil (1997) defined NGOs as 'self-governing, private, not-for-profit organisations that are geared to improving the quality of life for disadvantaged people' (1997: 2060). This definition can be useful in distinguishing NGOs from other third sector organisations such as trade unions.

Trade Union Cooperation with NGOs

The literature on NGOs is extensive, especially covering their work on gender and other strands such as disability or age; on diversity; on empowerment and participation (Fernando and Heston, 1997); and on policy-related advocacy (Visvanathan, 1997). However not much has been written about collaborations between trade unions and NGOs. As Arenas et al. note that 'this has attracted so little attention … despite its capital importance in Corporate Social Responsibility debates' (2009: 179) but this can relate to lack of discussion between the labour movement and the issues related to the topic of Corporate Social Responsibility (CSR) (Egels-Zanden and Hyllman, 2007). NGOs and trade unions are both civil society actors and what they have in common is a specific agenda and strategy aimed at the improvement of society: although trade unions are formed to represent the interests of their members, in the long run they also work on wider issues such as civil and democratic rights, equality or for the elimination of poverty – to name but a few examples. Such actions aim to improve the well-being of people and society as a whole. This interest is what they have in common with NGOs who also work towards the advancement of society and the improvement of living conditions. In this respect they have a common interest in joining forces to work more effectively in achieving their goals as both have become spokespersons for the protection of workers' rights, in the case of the former and for human rights, in the case of the latter (Eade, 2004). An example is the collaboration between the International Trade Union Confederation (ITUC) and Anti-Slavery International on a project entitled 'Never Work alone' which brings trade unions and NGOs together to work. A joint statement by Sharan Burrow, General Secretary of ITUC and Aidan McQuade, Director of Anti-Slavery International, on the collaboration by the two organisations, notes:

> the project started from the premise that while unions have extensive experience and expertise in promoting and protecting labour rights, specialised NGOs have also built up decades of experience in combating trafficking. Very rarely, however, have these two networks cooperated to address the symptoms and the causes of trafficking and forced labour on a national level. Therefore, the project intends to create a space to strengthen the links between trade unions and NGOs and identify the barriers and opportunities for joint work … The ITUC-Anti-Slavery project provides the opportunity for organisations to meet, discuss where such structural cooperation would be possible and desirable and begin the process of coalition/alliance building (ITUC, 2011).

This experience highlights the potentially useful collaboration between organisations in order to enhance understanding, develop more targeted action and create stronger links for further cooperation.

At international level, some authors have highlighted the importance of cooperation between unions and NGOs in their work on transnational corporations and worker rights, as the two types of organisation share common interests in fighting against the exploitation of workers, for example child labour or unfair wages or inhuman working conditions (Braun and Gearhart, 2004). Other research has shown how trade union – NGO cooperation has been central to workers' rights in factories in Guatemala, Mexico, the Dominican Republic, Sri Lanka and Indonesia (Egels-Zanden and Hyllman, 2007). However despite this positive outlook, cooperation between the two has met with resistance in the past, both from NGOs and trade unions respectively (Gallin, 2000, Anner and Evans, 2004). According to Gallin the growth in NGO organisations coincided with the gradual withdrawal of trade unions in the 1980s from a wide range of social concerns that they had been involved in the past, leaving a space for the emergence of 'issue oriented groups without traditional ties to labour' (2000: 19). In addition, globalisation processes gave rise and power to transnational corporations which led to a decline in core labour in services and manufacturing and the casualisation of production, through the employment of subcontractors. Gallin argues that as a result, and due to the weakening power of trade unions, there has been some tension or competition between unions and NGOs (Gallin, 2002).

Apart from differences in organising, Egels-Zanden and Hyllman (2011: 250) mention further obstacles to the cooperation between trade unions and NGOs, such as class differences, gender-related differences and differences in preferences for codes of conduct for NGOs and for international framework agreements for trade unions. Spooner (2004: 22–28) provides a comprehensive list of areas that can become potentially a problem in trade union and NGO collaborations. Some of these are relevant here and include, first, the diverse agendas of trade unions, consisting of different strategies and policies in responding to the issues and working conditions of the sectors they organise in and this can determine their willingness to seek cooperation with other organisations. For example agriculture unions work under conditions of low union density, where they may encounter child labour or workers with poor educational qualifications and in this case collaboration with an NGO can prove fruitful. In sectors, however, with strong unionised force of skilled workers, NGO cooperation may not be as high on the agenda. Second there is a difference between individual unions for example UNISON in the UK and national centres such as the TUC with the former representing workers to government and other governmental bodies, and the latter dealing with employers as social partners but not engaging in discussions in day to day terms and conditions, collective bargaining and union coordination. Therefore although unions have an important international role, they are actually defined also at the national and sub-national level (Herod, 2001). In this respect their needs are different and this can be seen by the nature of their collaborations with the different types of NGOs. Third, across Europe and the rest of the globe, there are substantial differences between the unions in terms of where they are located, whether in richer or poorer areas. This again can reflect the type of NGO they choose to collaborate with. A fourth issue is than of gender. In many cases unions are male dominated (Ford, 2006) especially at the level of leadership, even in unions with a large or majority female membership. Failure to address this imbalance may isolate them and damage the possibility of future collaborations with certain NGOs, especially those involved in programmes to support women. A fifth factor could be based on the governance and management of NGOs and trade unions, which include issues of transparency and accountability, information sharing and monitoring, as well as networking. This can connect to differences in class and culture but it can nevertheless pose a problem for collaborations. Sixth, is the issue of governance and democracy where trade unions may question the funding, credentials and legitimacy of an NGO, even in cases where they have interests in common. And finally is the issue of representation and advocacy and this could be a point of competing interests, as the traditional trade union role is to represent the interests of workers and they can be suspicious over the capacity of NGOs to do so (Roman, 2004) especially with regard to unorganised workers (Spooner, 2004). This last point was also raised in the Mapping study, as an interview with an NGO revealed:

> the cooperation with unions was until now rather difficult and selective. I would really appreciate it if unions saw NGOs as equal partners in opposing discrimination. Many people – in particular people we are representing – are not members of unions and are reluctant to approach unions with their discrimination experiences (Austria, NGO interviewee).

Braun and Gearhart (2004: 187–188) have identified three characteristics that differentiate human rights NGOs from trade unions and all three concern the way the two groups relate to power and influence their role in bringing social change: teleological, structural, and operational. *Teleological* refers to the difference between organisations 'driven by interest' (trade unions) or by 'ideals' (NGOs). As agencies trade unions have a specific interest in increasing their control over resources and decision-making, through their negotiations with businesses, either altering authority relations or shifting resources from owners to workers. On the contrary NGOs may present themselves as pursuing ideals without any material interest, other than their own self-preservation. An example from the Mapping study illustrates this point:

> Why do members do not signal problems with discrimination? They do in case of gender, age, trade union membership discrimination. There are no cases of sexual orientation

discrimination because people are too embarrassed to do so. In Poland there is no broader battle against sexual orientation discrimination except for NGOs. Trade unions should not be in the first line of the sexual orientation battle. We have our goals – salaries, working time, working conditions (Poland trade union interviewee).

However, as we saw in Chapter 5, Mapping study findings show that trans-national or cross-border cooperation between trade unions or cooperation between trade unions and NGOs gives strength to trade unions to confront 'hard' issues, for example when dealing with issues of homophobia or other positions that challenge the European equality agenda amongst their members. *Structural* differences are based on the fact that trade unions have members and are accountable to these members, and therefore their actions and bargaining responses need to meet the expectations of their members. The stronger the membership the more power trade unions have over corporate and public interest, as well as political power and the less likely their need to rely on NGOs. NGOs do not generally represent members and therefore they have the freedom to shape their strategies and follow their ideals without being accountable, apart from their need to build a reputation in order to survive. *Operational* differences refer to the way trade unions and NGOs relate to political power, and while NGOs remain outside politics and maintain the role of a watchdog, unions are more involved.

These three characteristics are useful in conceptualising differences between NGOs and trade unions but they also attract some criticism. For example the teleological differences are not so clear cut, as arguably trade union work is also based on ideals: that is the ideals of equality at workplace, the elimination of exploitation or of rights at work. The Mapping study provided many examples of trade union commitment to equality and social justice as a matter of one of their founding principles and trade union interviewees emphasised the importance of continuing to defend these during a period of economic crisis. The NGOs' independence can also be debated, as we have already noted they are not always financially independent and they also have to compete for resources. Similarly, in terms of membership, as mentioned earlier in this chapter, NGOs vary widely and larger NGOs tend to have some members that are players in the political arena, often internationally.

Partnership for Equality: Trade Union, NGOs and Equality Body Collaborations to Tackle Discrimination

The Mapping study gathered data on successful collaborations between trade unions and NGOs in fighting inequality based on the recognised anti-discrimination grounds. Chapter 5 presented findings on European level collaborations; here we review collaborations a at national level, as the study found a number of initiatives from each one of the strands of discrimination. Around half of the national experts noted a form of a trade union involvement with NGOs and/or equality bodies, although it was also reported that the presence of strong NGOs within a member state did not always guarantee that unions would be involved with them. For example, in Lithuania a considerable NGO activity was noted around discrimination issues, but there was no involvement of trade unions in that work. In the Czech Republic, the national expert found little evidence of trade union involvement in wider policy making with a focus on negotiations in large firms. In the Former Yugoslav Republic of Macedonia there was also growing NGO activity but no evidence of trade union engagement with them. A similar situation was reported from Bulgaria. Table 6.1 shows the distribution of collaborative programmes between trade unions and NGOs in the different geographical areas that the Mapping study found.

Out of the 23 initiatives that involved trade unions working with NGOs, the weakest cooperation levels were reported in Central and Eastern European member states (one out of 23), followed by five in Northern region, six Pan European and 11 in Southern Europe. Mendelson and Glenn (2002) found that although there was a plethora of NGOs operating in Central and Eastern European countries often they were part of larger organisations from Western Europe and as a result they tended to serve the interests of foreign donors, rather than those of the local community and local populations, raising questions on Spooner's (2004) point on governance and democracy. Similarly Leontidou (2010) argues that political instability, civil wars and experiences of dictatorships have contributed to a north – south divide in Europe in relation to civil societies, the welfare state, planning and grassroots mobilisations although findings in the Mapping study suggest that the majority of collaborative initiatives between trade unions and NGOs were concentrated in the Southern region.

One example of trade union and NGO cooperation in Romania there was the cooperation between the National Confederation of Trade Unions Cartel Alfa (CNS Cartel Alfa) and the Centre for Partnership and Equality, which led

Table 6.1   Collaborative programmes between trade unions and NGOs in different geographical regions

Southern region	11
Pan European	6
Northern region	5
Central and Eastern European	1
Total	23

to two projects based on partnerships with NGOs and other organisations, working around anti-discrimination training. In Portugal a manifesto for equal opportunities had been launched by the unions and supported by 14 key NGOs. In Malta the United Workers' Union (UHM) worked closely with a national disability commission and with a Migrants' Solidarity Movement. It also worked with the Malta Gay Rights movement (MGR) and at the time of the Mapping study had been planning to hold a one day seminar with MGR, aimed at trade union officials, discussing collective bargaining and LGBT rights. And in Luxembourg there was a long-standing partnership with NGOs supporting disabled people, activities which owed their origins to trade union support.

Joint action between trade unions and NGOs took a variety of forms as the following case study examples illustrate and resulted in a wider change of trade union policies and actions in the case of Poland; a better understanding of the need cover all forms of diversity within the union's equality agenda in the case of Belgium; improvement of work conditions and increased membership in the case of Italy; and exchange of good practice by bringing together employers, trade unions, governmental bodies, researchers and NGOs in the case of Slovenia.

Case Study Examples D

Example 1: wider change of trade union policies

This is an example of two trade union initiatives in Poland: The first was developed by ZNP (a teachers' union) in 2006, in collaboration with the NGO KPH (the Campaign Against Homophobia), to support LGBT teachers. The joint initiative was developed on a common strategy and helped ZNP to promote equality within the union itself and to prepare an ethical code which incorporates sexual orientation. The second initiative was developed by the OPZZ (Confederation) in 2009 and created a gay and lesbian officer post, an idea promoted by an OPZZ officer who was also a KPH activist and who had trade union work experience in the UK. Influenced by the work of UNISON on LGBT issues, the officer encouraged the adoption of a similar strategy in the OPZZ itself. For the OPZZ, support for LGBT initiatives meant a potential increase in union membership, as well as recognition of the prominence which LGBT issues have been given at a European trade union level. The two initiatives were developed within a strong homophobic climate and consequently attracted some homophobic criticism. This led to a continuous campaign by the ZNP to raise awareness on LGBT issues and in both cases the initiatives contributed to a wider change in union policies aimed at altering consciousness on LGBT issues while underlining the fact that homophobic attitudes at the workplace are a violation of labour law.

Example 2: incorporating all forms of diversity in the union's equality agenda

The Belgian Christian Trade Union confederation (CSC) engaged with relevant NGOs to respond to the needs of mainly Muslim workers in relation to working hours; accommodation; time for prayer, particularly during Ramadan; the wearing of the hijab; prayer areas; halal meals; days off for Muslim holidays; and leave to undertake a pilgrimage to Mecca. Traditionally the union had processed similar cases on an individual basis but, in collaboration with a Muslim NGO, an initiative was introduced at the local public hospital in Verviers to allow an area for prayer for Muslims. The union assisted with the negotiation process which resulted to the establishment, in 2008, of a meditation area open to all philosophies and religions. This outcome encouraged a debate around religion in the workplace at a trade union committee meeting where the delegates were asking for concrete solutions. It also raised awareness of religion as an important dimension of diversity. Religion was also to be included in the agendas of the monthly diversity group meetings of the CSC that brought together diversity advisers from Brussels and the Walloon area.

Example 3: improved work conditions and increased membership

The Italian General Confederation of Workers' Trade Unions (CGIL) introduced a number of initiatives in the area of LGBT rights, as a response to homophobia in the Italian society and in the area of racial/ethnic origin discrimination to respond to the tightening of immigration laws. CGIL adopted different approaches: the development of internal skills, in the case of 'traditional' discriminations (race, gender and disability) and a networking approach based on activities with external NGOs and community associations, in the case of 'new' forms of discrimination (sexual orientation and religion). More specifically in the area of LGBT issues there was an agreement with Arcigay, an LGBT NGO, on changing perceptions in the union and in the workplace which resulted in the development of a guide on the rights of LGBT workers, a 'glossary of terms' and training courses. The Calliope project – coordinated by Arcigay and the Gay Help Line and financially supported by the CGIL Lazio Region – was aimed at designing a training programme for women to increase awareness of discrimination on the grounds of sexual orientation and gender identity. The CGIL also introduced organisational changes with specific structures dedicated to immigration and disability issues and a 'New rights' section was created with the aim of coordinating different theme-based departments on the subject of sexual orientation and gender identity. At local level, it established 'New rights' desks, whose management generally was outsourced to gay rights' associations. The work of the CGIL and the two other confederations forced the government to fully transpose the directive by amending the law. CGIL reported that the use of traditional union methods and engagements with NGOs contributed to a better quality of life for workers who had experienced of discrimination while increasing the number of migrants and young workers in its membership. The large number of events organised jointly with NGO organisations and civil associations throughout the years contributed to the development and consolidation of local networks that had organised against renewed attacks on ethnic minority workers.

Example 4: exchange of good practice

Since 2004, the Slovenian Association of Free Trade Unions (ZSSS) has been active in combating LGBT discrimination at work with, amongst its main activities, participation in the 'Partnership for equality' project (between 2004 and 2007) under the EQUAL programme and a partnership with the NGO Društvo Škuc (Lesbian section – LL) and the Employers' Association of Slovenia (Združenje delodajalcev Slovenije – ZDS). Participation in 'Partnership for equality' encouraged further projects with the same partners, for example 'Diversity management in employment' (2008–2009) and cooperation with the ETUC on LGBT issues. The involvement of trade unions and employers, as partners in the project, had contributed to the development and implementation of anti-discrimination policies for an inclusive and safe work environment and equal opportunities and encouraged the exchange of good practices with transnational partners. Bringing together employers, trade unions, governmental public bodies, researchers and NGOs working against discrimination on grounds of sexual orientation, the network TRACE (Transnational Cooperation for Equality) was established with LGBT non-governmental organisations from different European countries – France, Lithuania, Slovenia and Sweden. The TRACE network produced a range of awareness-raising materials and training activities, such as the brochures 'Open up your workplace and norms at work', TV commercials that were shown on national TV stations and 13 regional seminars for trade unions and employers.

Reasons for Collaboration

The Mapping study found two prime reasons for enhanced cooperation between trade unions and NGOs in their work for equality and diversity: support from the European Commission or the European organisations and international level cooperation.

European support: At European level (see Chapter 5) cooperation between civil society organisations was quite advanced and specifically designed programmes had been put in place to facilitate this cooperation. In many cases European level cooperation provided legitimation and acted as an impetus for nationally based unions and NGOs to seek closer relations. For example the 'Open Door' programme of the Democratic Labour Federation (DEOK) in Cyprus was funded by EQUAL and brought together unions, NGOs, the equality body and government agencies to work together to enhance the participation of women in economic life, by encouraging businesses to adopt family-friendly policies and through the promotion of the reconciliation of professional and family life. Similarly the General Confederation of Greek Workers (GSEE) in Greece reported that it had well-developed links with other bodies, including NGOs, especially those working on migrant workers, on gender inequalities and on anti-racism and this cooperation was also the result of participating in EQUAL which remained as strong after the end of the programmes (see also Chapter 5 and the case study above).

International level cooperation: According to Spooner:

> Historically, trade unions have argued that a consistent defence of their members' interests demands a long-term struggle for a social and political context at national and international levels that is favourable to the wellbeing of people and society as a whole. They legitimately claim to be serving the interests of society in general, as would NGOs, in acting on the desire to advance and improve the human condition (Spooner, 2004: 19).

The Public Sector Union (DELTA) in Norway reported that they had close links with NGOs abroad, including in Russia, Zimbabwe and Lithuania, working together to develop a shelter for children and assisting staff to form a trade union and enhance their negotiating power. In Lithuania the union helped built a trade union for fire fighters. In some cases links were being developed between trade unions and international NGOs for a sector-focused purpose. For example the Italian UiL's Federation of Education Workers (UiL Scuola) had collaborated with Fondazione Sud (an NGO working for the development of the South) on the project 'Brazil-Italy Dialogue, providing training for teachers and trainers of the San Paolo Municipality'. Other forms of collaboration between trade unions and NGOs had been taking place at a local level but with a wider and international outcome, for example the Polish Teachers' Union

(ZNP) had collaborated with an NGO working for the protection of children and had raised money for children in Bieslan and Afghanistan. In some cases the conceptual differences between trade unions and NGOs, discussed above, were not as clear cut nor was their determination for collaboration. The study found examples of NGOs being established by trade unions that had been seeking to promote links at international level and, more particularly, with the developing world. Here we present all four examples, each of which demonstrates the scope for such work. One example was focused on cross-regional, cross-border cooperation, where a Spanish trade union sought links with a particular region in Africa, as a strategy to strengthen trade union activity but also to enable it to approach migrant workers; the Workers's Union (USOC) in Spain had created an NGO specialised in cooperation with Africa and had worked for the strengthening of trade unions there. Another example, that relates to international anti-discrimination work, was the case of a regional Spanish trade union in Andalusia which had set up a foundation called 'paz y solidaridad' to help women trade unionists in Latin America. The funding was assured through the yearly festival 'Entresures'. Similarly *Nexus*, an NGO created by the Italian General Confederation of Labour (CGIL), had commenced its life as a committee of the CGIL and had the role of working to create and support cooperation projects for socio-economic development in developing countries. Since 1991 Nexus had operated as an independent organisation, supported by fully paid staff, as well as volunteers, and had organised events to publicly discuss discrimination issues. The fact that the organisation had operated for over 20 years suggested that it represented a sustainable strategy. To summarise, findings from the Mapping study identified four main forms of international collaboration between trade unions and NGOs. First, general links between national trade unions and NGOs abroad with no particular action but ready to collaborate if a situation arose; second, sectorally focused collaborations to develop exchange of knowledge and training within the same sector; third, collaborations between national trade unions and national NGOs but at the level of international activity in order to fund-raise and help disadvantaged people in poverty-stricken or war-stricken countries; and fourth a union strategy to establish an NGO with the long-term purpose of independent activity, as a way of achieving closer links with other countries or regions.

The majority of the initiatives involving work based on partnerships existed mainly at a national level, eight of which were based on campaigning. For example in Luxemburg one trade union had worked closely with an NGO to provide support for technical and practical problems; an example mentioned was on transport for disabled people. The interviewee to the Mapping study stated that the outcome of such cooperation was more important than any differences that might have existed between partners: 'we work with other organisations even if we are not close politically with some of them'. In Italy, as the case study above shows, there has been a joint campaign activity between a union and a range of LGBT NGOs in order to raise awareness. There were also initiatives delivered through partnerships that took place at regional or local level, for example, in Spain the Secretariado Gitano Foundation (FSG), an NGO working with Roma communities, had long-standing collaborations with both the Trade Union Confederation of Workers' Commission (CCOO) and the General Workers' Union (UGT) at local level to tackle the widespread discrimination against Roma workers. The interviewee for the Mapping study believed that the NGO was in a good position to provide help, as Roma workers were not often in touch with trade unions, as they were suspicious of them. This collaboration provided mutual help between organisations; training schemes aimed at those advising Roma workers; training schemes for FSG staff on labour rights; the promotion of training among Roma workers; the enhancement of collective agreements, so that their content included a commitment to combating all kinds of discrimination; the organisation of awareness-raising campaigns; and mutual information to workers about the partners' activities. Another area of this cooperation – as this partnership included other organisations as well – was the development of a training programme on combating discrimination, mainly in the area of race and ethnicity. Regional or local trade union and NGO collaboration initiatives can also reflect the degree of integration at national level, regional and local levels, as these will differ in each Member State and within different stages of policy making (Foden, 1999). The Mapping study interviewee from the Polish Teachers' Union (ZNP) noted that its collaboration with the NGO Campaign Against Homophobia had assisted union strategy campaign against homophobia, to modernise its own strategy and to contribute to raising awareness about LGBT discrimination in the Polish society as a whole (see case study above). Finally, as in the previous case of *international level* cooperation, the Mapping study also found examples from Italy of active union participation in setting up NGOs as a means of campaigning for a particular issue and of raising awareness with the wider public. The Italian Union of Labour (UIL) was one of the founders of the National Youth Forum which comprised 80 youth organisations across the country. The idea for the establishment of this relatively new organisation was to lobby central government to increase the number of young people in strategic positions in politics or in central administration. Cooperation between trade unions and NGOs took place in order to enhance or utilise knowledge for a particular issue. For example the UiL Industry Federation of Food and Beverage (Uila-UiL) in Italy had developed, together with existing NGOs, a collaborative project entitled 'Speech to migrants' (La parola agli immigrant) which was carried out in 18 Italian provinces and involved both workers and employers in preparing a common questionnaire in order to gain a deeper understanding of discrimination experienced by migrant workers.

Conclusion

The chapter has discussed the degree of collaboration between trade unions and NGOs in working against discrimination in European societies. Existing literature has shown that the differences between the two types of organisation had contributed to an uneasy coexistence in the past. This was also fuelled by timing, as NGOs had become prominent during a time of political and membership decline for trade unions. However the two types of organisations have developed closer ties over time, while the promotion and strengthening of the concept of social dialogue in Europe has also revealed the benefits of possible cooperation. The Mapping study showed that collaboration between trade unions and NGOs had taken place as a result of three main factors. First the direct influence of the European Union, either through the influence of European level trade unions or as a result of EU funding for major projects. Second, as the result of general globalisation trends and migration movements that had encouraged unions to develop links with countries outside Europe, in order to carry out work in these countries or to develop better links with unions in these countries. NGOs had been vital to such an approach as an easier way of getting access to the new countries. The research also found evidence of trade unions helping to set up NGOs which functioned independently and helped carry out collaborative work in developing countries. Similar methods had also been used in the case of international level cooperation, as trade unions had also helped create NGOs within the national country as a strategy to expand union membership and create effective campaigning.

Chapter 7
Addressing Multiple Discrimination in the Workplace

Discrimination, like traffic through an intersection, may flow into one direction and it may flow into another. If an accident happens at an intersection, it can be caused by cars travelling from any number of directions, and, sometimes, from all of them. Similarly, if a black woman is harmed because she is in the intersection, her injury could result from sex discrimination or race discrimination (Crenshaw, 1989: 145).

Equal treatment is a recognised core principle of democratic values and at European level this is reflected in Article 21 of the Charter of Fundamental Rights of the European Union according to which discrimination on the grounds of:

> sex, race, colour, ethnic and social origin, genetic features, language, religion or belief, political or any other opinion, membership of a national minority, property, birth, disability, age or sexual orientation shall be prohibited.[1]

However, despite the presence of relevant legislation on equal treatment at both national and European levels, discrimination remains a persistent and widespread phenomenon in contemporary society and in the areas of work, education, health, welfare and social security. Discrimination manifests itself at both institutional and individual levels and contributes to social tensions and conflicts between majority and minority groups, leading to social unsettlement and disintegration. In its many forms, discrimination is likely to be the most frequently occurring human rights violation in Europe, as each year millions of people either have experiences or fear that they may become victims (Makkonen, 2007).

Much of the research on equality and on discrimination focuses on a single area, for example on gender or disability, and therefore treating cases of discrimination separately from one another. However, as the quotation above from Crenshaw (1989) suggests, people often are disadvantaged for more than one reason, for example for being a Black young person or a disabled, lesbian woman or a Muslim woman, wearing a headscarf. Therefore discrimination

---

1 see http://www.eucharter.org/home.php?page_id=28 (accessed in June 2014).

is often complex and reflects the multiple characteristics and identities which are part of a diverse society (Moon, 2006). In the last decade there has been a growing interest and awareness in the concept of multiple discrimination, which also started to appear in EU policy documents following the adoption of the two anti-discrimination Council Directives in 2000.

Although there has not yet been any binding EU legislation on the issue of multiple discrimination and the 2000 Council Directives do not contain any provisions for defining or prohibiting it, there has been discussion on the possibility of discrimination on more than one ground, for example in the case of women who are described as victims:

> in implementing the principle of equal treatment, the Community should, in accordance with Article 3(2) of the EC Treaty, aim to eliminate inequalities, and to promote equality between men and women, especially since women are often the victims of multiple discrimination (Council Directive 2000/78/EC).[2]

The same statement appears as Recital 14 in Council Directive 2000/43/EC.[3] However it is interesting that in the equal treatment between men and women in employment Council Directive 2004/113 and in Council Directive 2006/54[4] there is no mention of women as victims of multiple discrimination. Moreover, each Council Directive does provide that: 'Member States may introduce or maintain provisions which are more favourable to the protection of the principle of equal treatment than those laid down in this Council Directive' and therefore additional country-focused provisions are not contrary to the Council Directives, so long as they do not undermine the basic rights established under these Council Directives. In April 2009 the European Parliament introduced a number of amendments to the Commission's proposal for a Council directive on implementing the principle

---

2 http://eur-lex.europa.eu/legal-content/EN/TXT/?uri=CELEX:32000L0078 (accessed in May 2014).

3 Council Directive 2000/78: http://eur-lex.europa.eu/LexUriServ/LexUriServ. do?uri=CELEX:32000L0078:en:HTML and Racial Equality Council Directive 2000/43: http://eur-lex.europa.eu/LexUriServ/LexUriServ.do?uri=CELEX: 32000L0043:en:HTML (accessed in May 2014).

4 Council Directive 2004/113/EC of 13 December 2004 implementing the principle of equal treatment between men and women in the access to and supply of goods and services and Council Directive 2006/54/EC of the European Parliament and of the Council of 5 July 2006 on the implementation of the principle of equal opportunities and equal treatment of men and women in matters of employment and occupation. For more information see Countouris, N. and Freedland, M. (2012) *The personal scope of the EU sex equality Council Directives,* European network of legal experts in the field of gender equality, European Commission.

of equal treatment (Council Directive COM (2008) 426) which added a provision for multiple discrimination:

According to Article 1, multiple discrimination occurs when discrimination is based:

(a) on any combination of the grounds of religion or belief, disability, age, or sexual orientation, or

(b) on any one or more of the grounds set out in paragraph 1, and also on the ground of any one or more of

   – (i) sex (in so far as the matter complained of is within the material scope of Directive 2004/113/EC as well as of this Directive)

   – (ii) racial or ethnic origin (in so far as the matter complained of is within the material scope of Directive 2000/43/EC as well as of this Directive), or

   – (iii) nationality (in so far as the matter complained of is within the scope of Article 12 of the EC Treaty).[5]

The above definition can be viewed as a positive outcome in the protection against discrimination, as it ensures that cases of multiple discrimination can be also addressed and that claims of discrimination can be based on a combination of the grounds covered by EU anti-discrimination legislation. However there are certain restrictions: first, the proposals do not include the combination of gender and racial/ethnic discrimination; and second the proposals do not cover multiple discrimination within employment and this may have a negative impact in Member States where courts have already recognised multiple discrimination on the combined grounds of gender and racial/ethnic discrimination within employment (Burri and Schiek, 2009).

This chapter focuses on the concept of 'multiple discrimination' within the area of equality and diversity and discusses the usefulness of the concept both as an analytical tool and as a way of strengthening the case against discrimination. The first part of the chapter looks at the development of the concept especially within the academic socio-legal debates. These sprang from the black feminist movement, mainly in the US, and were concentrated on the use of the term of intersectionality, which in literature often came to be used interchangeably with the term multiple discrimination. The second part concentrates on the development of relevant policies, especially in relation to trade unions.

---

5 Article 1: P_6 TA (2009)0211: http://www.europarl.europa.eu/sides/getDoc.do?pubRef=-//EP//TEXT+TA+P6-TA-2009–0211+0+DOC+XML+V0//EN (accessed in May 2014).

Background

Multiple discrimination as a concept attracted academic interest relatively recently as it was explored by socio-legal scholars in the 1980s, albeit the term was not recognised as a clear legal term. Black American feminists in the late 1970s, for example the Combahee River Collective, a black lesbian feminist organisation, had raised the argument around the presence of 'interlocking systems of oppression', advocating the existence of racial-sexual oppression where race, class and sex oppression are experienced simultaneously and not separately by black women (Combahee River Collective, 1982: 13–22). Scholars such as Davis (1981), Giddings (1984) and Lorde (1998) also drew attention to the inadequacy of the single ground approach to legislation to cover inequalities experienced by black women because of their ethnicity and gender. The conjuncture of gender and race was further developed as a concept by bell hooks as she criticised the common discourse used in feminist political theory and argued that the two are inseparable identity characteristics that distinguish black women from black men and black women from white women:

> From the onset of my involvement with the women's movement I was disturbed by the white women's liberationists' insistence that race and sex were two separate issues. My life experience had shown me that the two issues were inseparable, that at the moment of my birth, two factors determined my destiny, my having been born black and my having been born female (bell hooks, 1981: 12).

bell hooks also discusses the importance of the fact that:

> despite the reality that white upper and middle class women in America suffer from sexist discrimination and sexist abuse, they are not as a group as oppressed as poor white or black or yellow women. Their unwillingness to distinguish between various degrees of discrimination caused black women to see them as enemies. As many upper middle class white feminists who suffer least from sexist oppression were attempting to focus all attention on themselves, it follows that they would not accept an analysis of woman's lot in America which argued that not all women are equally oppressed because some women are able to use their class, race and educational privilege to effectively resist sexist oppression (bell hooks, 2000: 383).

With this statement bell hooks brings a strong element of class and race into her analysis and argues for the need to understand the different degrees of discrimination experienced by different groups as not all women are equally oppressed.

In the late 1980s the American legal scholar Kimberle Crenshaw, together with a number of other scholars, adopted a Critical Race Theory approach and introduced the concept of intersectionality as a theoretical framework to better understand and analyse the complex and interrelated forms of power, according to which black women experience 'double-discrimination' on the basis of race and sex simultaneously. The main argument has been that individuals in general can belong to more than one disadvantaged minority group and as a result they can experience a more specific form of discrimination based on these multiple characteristics (Crenshaw, 1989). This approach identified an analytical weakness in a single category perspective. In her critique Crenshaw argues that:

> It becomes more apparent how dominant conceptions of discrimination condition us to think about subordination as disadvantage occurring along a single categorical axis. I want to suggest further that this single axis framework erases Black women in the conceptualization, identification and remediation of race and sex discrimination by limiting inquiry to the experiences of otherwise privileged members of the group (1989: 139–40).

As well as a method of scholarly analysis, Crenshaw also saw intersectionality as a tool for policy making and introduces the distinction between structural and political intersectionality. Accordingly, structural intersectionality covers the way in which the intersections of race, gender, class and immigration status are experienced by people. In the area of employment structural intersectionality can explain why for example a black woman experiences barriers to jobs that mainly employ white women or jobs that are mainly for men. According to Verloo (2006: 213) relevant questions in analysing structural intersectionality include: 'How and when does racism amplify sexism? How and when does class exploitation reinforce homophobia? How and when does homophobia amplify racism?'

Political intersectionality on the other hand covers the interaction of inequalities and the way this is addressed by the political institutions and strategies (Krizsan et al., 2012). For Verloo the main questions for analysing political intersectionality include:

> How and where does feminism marginalize ethnic minorities or disabled women?
> How and where do measures on sexual equality or on racism marginalize women?
> How and where do gender equality policies marginalize lesbians? (2006: 213).

Both Crenshaw (1991) and Collins (2000) advocated that intersectionality could potentially include further social divisions than race, gender and class which traditionally have been the focus of most researchers, whether or not they adhered to the model of `triple oppression' (Yuval-Davis, 2006).

The concept was developed further during the 1990s through various theories such as transnational feminism and the relevance of race and class (Mohanty,

1992), post colonialism and the diasporic experiences of Asian women (Brah, 1996), the interrelation between capitalism and patriarchy (Sargent, 1981) or notions of power:

> ... an effective analysis requires exploring how subordinations are linked to produce diverse outcomes with regard to the placement of collective subjects within the different major divisions that construct them (Anthias and Davis, 1992: 20).

As movements on racial and sexual equality rights developed during the 1970s, other scholars included in their analysis additional social divisions such as age, sexuality, cultural differences, ability or faith and religion (Bradley, 1996). More recently other minorities such as disabled people, members of the LGBT community, young people or older people have started to discuss their disadvantages on more than one ground and as a dimension of their multiple identities. Consequently multiple discrimination has become increasingly more recognised and includes more combinations, such as disability and sexual orientation or gender and age. However the economic crisis throughout Europe can fuel multiple discrimination, just as it is challenging for the equalities agenda in general, as, for example, when members of minority disadvantaged groups are more likely to lose their jobs first.[6]

Multiple Discrimination in the Area of Equality: Theoretical Framework

Despite weaknesses in terms of its legislative base, there is a growing interest in a multiple discrimination approach, both within academic and policy making circles and as a result there is a rising international recognition of the concept, for example, the Beijing Declaration, Fourth World Congress on Women (1995) noted that the Congress would:

> Intensify efforts to ensure equal enjoyment of all human rights and fundamental freedoms for all women and girls who face multiple barriers to their empowerment and advancement because of such factors as their race, age, language, ethnicity, culture, religion, or disability, or because they are indigenous people ...[7]

---

6 European Union Agency for Fundamental Rights (2010) *The impact of the Racial Equality Directive – views of trade unions and employers in the European Union: strengthening the fundamental rights' architecture in the EU IV*, Luxembourg.

7 http://www.un.org/womenwatch/daw/beijing/platform/declar.htm (accessed in April 2014).

The Committee on the Elimination of Racial Discrimination has declared that 'that racial discrimination does not always affect women and men equally or in the same way'. And more recently multiple discrimination was recognised in the UN World Conference against Racism, Racial Discrimination, Xenophobia and Related Intolerance held in Durban, South Africa in 2001:

> We recognize that racism, racial discrimination, xenophobia and related intolerance occur on the grounds of race, colour, descent or national or ethnic origin and that victims can suffer multiple or aggravated forms of discrimination based on other related grounds.

Two main reasons have been discussed in relation to the growing interest in multiple discrimination debate and research. First, and as mentioned above, due to the rising awareness of the pluralisation of society and the growth of identity politics in the 1970s, taking its example from the civil rights' movement and the social mobilisation around discriminated collective identities based on race/ethnicity, religion, gender, sexuality, disability, age becoming part of the political landscape (Kenny, 2004: 3). Second is the emergence of what Vertovec (2007) called super-diversity which is the result of global migration movements. The term captures the complexity of diversity in modern societies and includes the additional variables needed to better understand it. These can include three components, country of origin (with features such as ethnicity, language, religious tradition, regional and local identities, cultural values and practices), migration channel (gendered flows, specific social networks and particular labour market niches), and legal status (determining a hierarchy of entitlements and restrictions).

Multiple discrimination refers to discrimination against groups based on more than one identity characteristic and 'the more a person differs from the norm, the more likely she is to experience multiple discrimination and the less likely she is to gain protection' (Fredman, 2005: 14). Some examples of multiple discrimination can include a Muslim woman being made redundant because she refuses to remove her headscarf or a female migrant worker who is active in a trade union and experiences harassment from the employer or an HIV positive gay man being dismissed from his position. What these examples have in common is the lack of an effective legal protection that takes into account the multiple identity of the individual and the experiences of discrimination based on these multiple characteristics. In this respect in such cases individuals may experience deeper discrimination and prejudice placing them in a vulnerable situation in employment but also other areas of social life. Fredman (2005) argues that reluctance to legislate for multiple discrimination is based on fears of opening the Pandora's box in terms of claims by numerous subgroups.

A Stonewall study on understanding prejudice in the UK identified four minority groups against whom respondents most frequently expressed prejudice: refugees and asylum seekers; travellers and Roma; people from ethnic minorities; and gay or lesbian people. However regarding multiple discrimination the report concluded that awareness of discrimination on more than one ground is low and recommended that organisations that represent minority groups should be more proactive in identifying and making multiple discrimination more visible (Valentine and McDonald, 2004: 13). Research on homophobia by the FRA showed that people from ethnic minorities are at risk of being discriminated on the grounds of sexual orientation and gender within their ethnic community and on the grounds of race and ethnicity within the LGBT community. The research also found that LGBT people with disabilities had problem accessing LGBT venues or meeting places and some LGBT people in care, such as disabled or older LGBT people suffer stereotyping and exclusion by other residents.[8] Equally research on LGBT issues found a strong element of multiple discrimination in the experiences of members of the LGBT group, for example young people experienced bullying and harassment in school, Black and Minority Ethnic (BME) workers were reluctant to come out at the workplace and disabled people felt isolated and excluded from both LGBT and disabled communities (Colgan et al., 2006). There is also a growing interest in the application of intersectional discrimination in the study of age, as according to Roseberry (2011), aging in modern societies is often linked to disability especially in the area of employment. For example studies have shown that older workers may face stereotyped views that they are less productive, less motivated and less likely to accept change or to receive training while there is little evidence to support these perceptions. Intellectual decline is often linked to more general health issues and little evidence has been found to support the assumption that older workers do not accept change or that they cannot learn to perform new tasks because of their age (ibid.). Louise Richardson, Vice-President of AGE, representing AGE Platform Europe stated at an Equality Summit: 'There is an urgent need to address the serious problem of age discrimination, in particular for specific groups of older people who face discrimination on account not only of their age but due to other factors such as disability, race, ethnicity or/and sexual orientation'.[9]

Various terms have been engaged to understand the complexity of discrimination and include 'additive' 'compound' and 'intersectional'. In international documents, the term 'multiple discrimination' is used as a broad

---

8 Cited in *Destination Equality* Magazine, Winter 2010–2011, published by ILGA: www.ilga-europe.org/content/download/18974/ … /magazine_WWW.pdf (accessed in May 2014).

9 http://www.age-platform.eu/news-press/age-a-the-media/age-communication-to-the-media-press-releases/1574-multiple-discrimination-in-old-age-a-neglected-issue (accessed in May 2014).

term to describe both additive discrimination and intersecting discrimination (Sheppard, 2011) and often these terms are used interchangeably (Makkonen, 2002) and 'in different ways, sometimes inconsistently and with ambiguity' (Phoenix and Pattynama, 2006: 118). As it has been argued above, multiple discrimination is a generic term that defines a situation where discrimination can occur due to a variety of separate characteristics. It is usually based on the view that particular groups in society are more vulnerable. For example discrimination against older women can be understood as discrimination on the grounds of gender and in addition on the grounds of age. It is possible therefore for a person to be discriminated against on more than one ground on any occasion but the different grounds can still be distinguished (Burri, S. and Schiek 2009: 3). This implies that, for the purpose of analysis, discrimination based on more than one ground which preserves their own characteristics (Hannett, 2003) and multiple discrimination can be separated into components of recognised characteristics (Abrams 1994: 2482–2492). This concept has been criticised by feminists like Crenshaw (1992) or Spelman (1988) who argue that it is not helpful to disentangle the different grounds:

> It is highly misleading to say, without further explanation, that Black women experience 'sexism and racism'. It suggests that Black women experience one form of oppression as Blacks (the same thing Black men experience) and that they experience another form of oppression as women (the same thing white women experience) (Spelman 1988: 122).[10]

Additive or compound discrimination on the other hand refers to a situation where a person experiences discrimination on more than one ground simultaneously and these discriminations accumulate to become a distinct discrimination experience for the individual (Sheppard, 2011). An example could be the policy of an organisation to recruit women with a certain height and a successful written exam. This may be indirect discrimination based on ethnicity, gender and nationality, as some migrant women may not have the asked-for height or may not speak the language of the host country well enough to pass the exam (Gerards, 2007). Unlike the previous situation here it is not possible to separate the various grounds of the additive or compound discriminations, which is a common feature with the third approach of intersectionality. However theorists have also critiqued the compound discrimination approach as they believe that it is not one ground of discrimination accumulating on another that produces a distinctive form of discrimination. Instead it is the interaction between several

---

10 Cited in Roseberry, L. (2011) 'Multiple discrimination', in Sargeant, M. *Age discrimination and diversity: multiple discrimination from an age perspective*, Cambridge University Press, Cambridge.

grounds which operate together and therefore it is not possible to distinguish which of the grounds is dominant in any situation (Spelman 1988). For this reason the additive/compound approach is often based on one level of analysis – the experiential – and does not allow for differentiation between different levels (Yuva-Davis, 2006).

Intersectionality as a term originated, as we saw earlier, in the Black feminist movement in America and has been widely used in academic work in recent years. The term refers to the operation and interaction of different strands of discrimination in such a way that first, it is not possible to separate them and second, they create a new and complex form of discrimination (Schieck, 2011) where the different characteristics interact and in combination they reinforce discriminations and prejudice (Lewis, 2010). As Anthias and Yuval Davis (1983:62–63) note:

> … race gender and class cannot be tagged onto each other mechanically for as concrete social relations, they are enmeshed in each other and the particular intersections involved produce specific effects.

Some representative examples of intersectional discrimination are the cases of female migrants from different ethnicities or older, disabled women. There are three main elements in the intersectional theory. First intersectionality does not demonstrate the role of each of the discrimination grounds involved and its contribution to the overall discrimination experienced by people. Second, intersectional discrimination often affects women more than men. And third, it often appears to be linked to structural and institutional causes (Makkonen, 2002). The concept has been criticised for its methodological complexity but also for its focus on interlocking power relations, without considering the 'production of hierarchies among the different relationships of power and domination in place' making it a descriptive anti-racist and post-colonial approach (Erel et al., 2010: 281). In terms of legislation one of the main criticisms of anti-discrimination law is that it has been developed on a single ground approach. *Bahl v the Law Society, UK [2004] IRLR 799*, a case before the UK courts, illustrates this point. Ms Bahl, an Asian woman claimed that she had been subject to discriminatory treatment both on the grounds of her race or ethnic origin and of her gender. The Employment Tribunal ruled that she could be compared to a white man, so that the effect of her race and her sex could be considered. However, both the Employment Appeal Tribunal and the Court of Appeal ruled that this was not possible because each ground had to be disaggregated, separately considered, and a ruling made on it, even if the claimant had experienced them as inextricably linked'.[11] As Kotkin (2009) notes for the US:

---

11 cited in Burri and Schiek (2006: 15): ec.europa.eu/social/BlobServlet? docId=776&langId=en (accessed in May 2014).

Despite the common sense notion that the more 'different' a worker is, the more likely she will encounter bias, empirical evidence shows that multiple claims – which may account for more than 50 per cent of federal court discrimination actions – have even less chance of success than single claims ... the more complex the claimant's identity, the wider must be cast the evidentiary net to find relevant comparative, statistical, and anecdotal evidence (Kotkin in Burri and Schiek, 2009: 7).

We can therefore conclude that the courts and legal systems need to become more accommodating to the growing body of social science research in multiple discrimination and intersectionality, in order to better assist victims of multiple discrimination. This is an area on anti-discrimination legislation that will need to adapt to the complexities and diversities of contemporary society no matter how challenging this is.

To conclude, this section has looked at the theoretical framework and uses of multiple discrimination which came to the forefront of academic and policy debates during the 1980s. The concept originates in the experiences of black women in America as well as in the civil rights movement itself which gave rise to a discussion of different identities as we saw in Chapter 2. Multiple discrimination as a concept is now widely used by social, legal, political and human rights scholars, who use different terms to describe the experiences of discrimination on more than one ground. In terms of legislation, in many EU Member States there is insufficient protection for victims of multiple discrimination and while at EU level multiple discrimination is increasingly being referenced in documents and in EU funded research, there are no legally binding provisions that take into account a combination of identity characteristics.

Multiple Discrimination and Trade Unions

As was discussed in the previous chapters, the Mapping study concentrated primarily on the different strands of discrimination recognised by the Council Directive 2000/78 which established a general framework for equal treatment in accessing employment and while in work, together with the Council Directive 2000/43. The concept of multiple discrimination was utilised in the Mapping study to identify any interrelations between the different strands and to explore the type of equality and diversity provisions offered by the trade unions. It was found that the term multiple discrimination itself was relevant for three reasons. First the term was being used to look at the relationship between the different strands of inequalities in trade unions and in relation to their equality policies. Second, the concept was used to analyse some of the findings. Third, it was useful to understand how multiple discrimination had been conceptualised and reflected on in the planning of trade union equality initiatives, since they had focused on tackling inequalities at all levels of society. The study assumed that discrimination is both substantial and widespread in European societies and therefore that it could be understood without reflecting on the certain complexities of inequality itself. And as the Mapping study was located both within an academic discussion and social policy making, it used the concept of multiple discrimination – rather than intersectionality – as a more commonly referenced term to policy making and in more generic analytical way rather than as a specific issue.

Relation between Different Strands in Trade Union Policies

A general finding in the research was that the cases of multiple discrimination were limited and that when present the difficulties in tackling them and the need for further work in this area was emphasised by respondents to the Mapping study. Most trade union official interviewees did not have a clear understanding of the concept, of its usefulness in the planning and designing initiatives or of its policy implications. Eighteen of the 130 initiatives examined covered all grounds of discrimination; however this did not mean that trade union officials recognised the concept of multiple discrimination, rather it meant that their initiative or project had a more general approach towards discrimination and therefore included more than one strand. The majority of initiatives across the EU dealt with single strand cases of discrimination or they were in favour of fighting discrimination in a more general way rather than in focusing on specific strands. It was found that priority was given to the primary aim of the unions, in the negotiation of favourable work conditions for workers, associated with wider claims for equality, equal opportunities and social justice, and that any claims such as the right not to be discriminated against on the basis of 'race', gender, sexuality, disability, age, belief or religion, become secondary (Alberti et al., 2013: 4134). The following statement illustrates the point:

> In such cases of multiple discrimination we try to disentangle the different grounds of discrimination. However according to my opinion too much analysis does not make sense because what is more important is to take concrete action and steps against discriminatory practices (Austria, trade union interviewee).

Low engagement with issues of multiple discrimination by the trade unions reflected the overall limitations in embracing the concepts and incorporating them as a main item in policy making, at both EU and member state levels. Moore et al. (2012) in their research on equality representatives in the UK made similar findings on the difficulties their respondent trade union representatives had in understanding the concepts.

In other cases it was acknowledged that a worker could be discriminated against on the basis of multiple characteristics, however, as discussed in the previous section, interviewees highlighted the restrictions in the legal systems and noted than in such cases it was easier to focus on one characteristic:

> … as mentioned [the union] has had five cases [of multiple discrimination] in the last three years. One of these cases involved a dismissal due to multiple discrimination, where an immigrant had problems with his arm and spoke poor Danish. The union chose to run the case on ethnicity and won the case in court (Denmark, trade union interviewee).

Again drawing on the limitations of the legal system some interviewees however reported that in certain cases discrimination factors were so entangled that they were difficult to both identify and separate:

> In the event of multiple discrimination the [union] policy was to pursue all discrimination strands separately, since the legislation currently required this, although it was difficult to tell in some cases where the real reason for the discrimination lay. Additionally the remedies provided for were different for different discriminations, for example the reasonable adjustment clause of the Disability Discrimination Act. The union did not prioritise any particular form of discrimination as a matter of principle (UK, trade union interviewee).

The last remark in this interview indicates the general trend of trade unions to tackle discrimination as a whole, rather than on different grounds. It also to an extent indicates an overall commitment to equality issues, as all forms of discrimination are being treated as an equal injustice to the victim.

Multiple Discrimination Initiatives

Despite the limitations for incorporating more fully the concept of multiple discrimination into the equality initiatives of trade unions in Europe, the Mapping study found that there had been cases specifically targeting discrimination on more than one level and in many of the examples the strand of disability accounted for one of the characteristics. As one trade union interviewee explained the union was often approached by victims regarding claims of discrimination relating to age and disability:

> … older workers with long working experiences and relatively high wages who are suffering from burn out or become chronically ill are asked to retire or are

getting humiliated at the workplace until they are ready to go (Austria, trade union interviewee).

Drawing on the weakness of the limitation of the legislative system and recognising the need for further action, an Italian trade unionist designed an initiative to specifically work on and enhance understanding of multiple grounds of discrimination:

> Together with our other eight national partners (also representing the other national confederation), the union at national level, is carrying out a project aimed at developing an integrated strategy to combat all forms of discrimination and [specifically] the double forms in which discrimination on the ground of race is combined to those based on religion or gender … in reaction to the weaknesses points of the Italian legislative system mentioned above, the objectives (Italy, trade union interviewee).

This initiative had incorporated a strong element of awareness-raising on the issue of discrimination where it was being experienced on more than one level. Other multiple discrimination initiatives were designed to overcome discrimination on the grounds of age and ethnicity. For example a Dutch union ran a campaign called 'Proud of your name' which was against anonymous job applications:

> … the reason for this project was the public call for anonymous applications which was supposed to create equal opportunities in job application procedures for ethnic minority youth. In 2006, there was much media attention for the idea that many young ethnic minorities were not invited to job interviews, whereas their native Dutch friends, with similar job application letters and CV's, did get invited. Some concluded that this was because ethnic minorities were being discriminated against because of their surnames (Netherlands, trade union interviewee).

Three more initiatives based on age (young) and disability had been developed by Dutch trade unions. On some occasions, although no specific multiple discrimination initiatives had been designed, trade unions proceeded in making structural changes in their organisation in order first to accommodate equalities and second to better understand the interaction between them:

> [the union] has what they call an 'Equality Team', which consists of three full-time employees on the minority area, two on the gender area, one on disability and social work and a half person on the area of sexual orientation. The Equality Team was established in 2004. They work together and that strengthens the case for multiple discrimination (Denmark, trade union interviewee).

Similar arrangements were referenced in the UK, as the Trades Union Congress (TUC) had introduced changes and provided reserved seats on the LGBT and disability committees to allow black, women and disabled members to be represented. And in Denmark a trade union introduced training to promote equality for young ethnic minority workers, illustrating the practicalities of delivering a multiple discrimination initiative.

Case study example E

The Timber and Construction Workers' Union in Denmark (TIB), introduced a trial pre-apprenticeship trainee programme, as the outcome of an agreement between the union and the employers' organisation. Discussions between the employers' association DST and the union led to the development of the programme which ran between 2005 and 2006 and focused on young ethnic minority people to help them acquire relevant skills and gain an insight into the industry, the companies and the professional, personal and the social skills required to successfully complete a vocational training course in this sector. The programme was based on the idea that young ethnic minority workers were under-represented in the sector with only few apprenticeships available, despite these being the main route of entry into this area of work. TIB took responsibility for finding suitable young people and DST had responsibility for finding companies willing to participate. The TIB visited local employment agencies and youth counsellors, as well as municipal primary and secondary schools to inform them of the project. The initiative was formally evaluated by the two organisations after a year of operation and it was decided not to continue it. Nevertheless the programme gave rise to requests for similar agreements from other employers in the sector, aimed at increasing the participation of young people generally and leading to further agreements between the TIB, the Confederation of Danish Industry and the Danish Construction Association. Additionally, the TIB signed an agreement with a secondary school, where the union was advising school students about work and apprenticeship in the crafts sector. The initiative involved the use of significant resources, both in terms of work input and finance for the TIB and the DST, although there was some financial assistance from the Danish Ministry of Integration. The initiative was viewed as a success and the TIB has publicised it in a special issue of its union journal, with an article on Pirasath Satkonam, a successful trainee.

Multiple discrimination trade union initiatives are often conceptualised through gender mainstreaming as noted by some of the national experts who participated in the Mapping study. For example, in Spain, initiatives on age discrimination were reported to also have a gender focus, as well as looking at the impact of age discrimination on women. In Austria an initiative by the trade union confederation and several other trade unions was implementing gender mainstreaming within union structures, with pilot projects on training and on public relations. As part of the initiative a booklet on gender mainstreaming had been published and contained best practice cases for gender mainstreaming in collective agreements. Equally in Belgium:

> [gender mainstreaming has] been identified as a priority and is being applied to all anti-discrimination policies. So in the reality, the women's commission of the FGTB pays attention to aged and ethnic minority women but not particularly to disabled women ... when there is a trade union committee, the women's commission controls that the balance is respected (Belgium, trade union interviewee).

Finally in Cyprus, a trade union in cooperation with other trade unions, constructed a programme to help develop action on older migrant workers, as they were identified as particularly vulnerable due to their precarious employment and lack of access to representation, thus:

> ... [the union] cooperates with other trade union organisations in the field of combating discrimination mostly in the framework of the social dialogue, as well as at other fora, such as for example parliamentary committees, when they are invited to submit their positions. One example of joint action cited by the respondent and currently under way is the right to organise in trade unions, which affects mostly people vulnerable to discrimination, such as migrants and older workers, men and women (Cyprus, trade union interviewee).

Conclusion

This chapter has discussed multiple discrimination in the context of trade union initiatives on equality and diversity. The first part of the chapter located the concept within the EU anti-discrimination legal provisions and argued that although there is a growing interest in the concept and that it is often mentioned in EU documentation, analysis and research, there is no legal protection for cases of multiple discrimination in either of the two European Council Directives (Council Directive 2000/43 on equal treatment irrespective of racial and ethnic origin and Council Directive 2000/78 on equal treatment in employment and occupation) or other legally binding legislation. Multiple discrimination has however been referenced in terms of a future Directive proposal, albeit only with respect to gender. The chapter looked next at the historical background to try and understand how the concepts came into being, how they evolved and why they are relevant to contemporary society. It has been argued that there has been a shift from a gender focused argument (as the concept first emerged within the black feminism discourse) to a more general interaction between the recognised forms of equality, itself reflecting the highly diverse contemporary societies characterised as super diverse by Vertovec (2007). The concept of multiple discrimination was then explored in terms of the theoretical frameworks and forms of multiple discrimination that have been developed within academic and policy making debates. The final part of the chapter discussed findings from the Mapping survey. The research found that there has been limited engagement with the concept of multiple discrimination by trade unions in Europe and this was reflected in the overall limited use of the concept, both in terms of legislation and in terms of society as a whole. In some cases trade unions were more likely to adopt a more traditional role and fight discrimination as a whole rather than on separate strands. Other cases showed a limited understanding of the concept itself and in others the weakness of the legal systems in protecting the victims of multiple discrimination was reflected in trade union policies. Multiple discrimination in many cases appeared to be conceptualised through a gender mainstreaming approach which had been adopted by the trade unions. In practical terms, other strands of discrimination had been combined with gender, such as gender and age, or gender and ethnicity or gender and disability to name some of the examples. As a concluding remark it can be argued that more awareness in needed in the area of multiple discrimination – especially during a period of economic crisis –and at how it can be addressed by policy makers as well as trade unions and in legal terms there is a need for a new legal structure to provide protection for the victims.

Chapter 8
Equality and Diversity under the Shadow of the Economic Crisis

> … resolving the current crisis without taking care to reduce income inequality is likely to leave in place the seeds for another crisis in the not-so-distant future, and also to damage the legitimacy of the European integration project (ETUI, 2012).

Europe today is going through a deepening economic downturn, one experienced by European society as a whole and to various degrees by each of the Member States. Since 2008 the impact of this economic crisis has become a central theme in the public political discourse for policy analysts, the media, experts and observers. The resulting Eurozone crisis features regularly on the front pages of national newspapers across Europe and much has been written about its intensity and its relevance to the political and social crisis which followed as a consequence. Criticism has been voiced about the democratic processes of decision-making, about the relevance of social dialogue, about the role of national politicians in dealing with the negative trends that the crisis has promoted and as the above quote suggests, about longer term policies. At the same time migration policies and inter-European mobility have become a paramount issue within the Member States, giving rise to xenophobia, racism and hostility to the further expansion of the European Union. In this context the European motto *United in our diversity*, which refers to the diversity of Member States and the unity within the framework of shared values, has been contested, as it is precisely this increasing diversity and difference that is now central to many of the debates within Europe, especially on the issue of migration and integration, particularly from right wing politicians and parts of the press. It can be argued that the Jeremy Rifkin's European dream of a Europe that would open up new opportunities and new possibilities at the forefront of the international arena is far from real in the current climate (Rifkin, 2004).

In terms of the social impact of the economic crisis, research has pointed to rising levels of social inequality between and within nations. A 2011 report by the OECD, *Divided we stand: why inequality keeps rising*, found that, within the OECD countries, income inequality had increased enormously in the last three decades, even during periods of economic growth but this trend had been particularly affected by the current economic crisis. The report also found that the average income of the richest 10% is now about nine times that of the poorest 10 % across the OECD countries and that, according to the latest trends, inequality grew more than anywhere else during the 2000s in those countries considered as traditionally low in inequality such as Germany, Denmark, and Sweden and the other Nordic countries (OECD, 2011). According to Harvey the persistence of such disparities can be explained by the domination of the neoliberal system:

> neo-liberalisation has not been effective in revitalizing global capital accumulation, but it has succeeded remarkably well in restoring, or in some instances (as in Russia and China) creating, the power of an economic elite which characterises the way the global capitalism is working today (2005: 19).

And in some respect the rise of neoliberalism as a contemporary economic system was embraced by governments across the globe and within the European Union and influenced social formations and political thinking while undermining trade unions, labour rights and welfare states expressing the political and economic will of the centre left and the right (Walby, 2013).

The OECD report (2011) identified four drivers for this trend, and although the study of inequality was limited to an examination of the wage gap, we would suggest that they are useful as they can relate to some of the discrimination strands covered by the Race and Ethnicity Directive 2000/43 and the Employment Equality Directive 2000/78. The first driver was changes in technology which in terms of employment had been particularly beneficial for highly skilled professionals, as the increase in the demand for skilled workers has outstripped the growth of their supply (Van Reenen, 2011). The second was the changes in working conditions, the increase in part-time jobs and the increase in non-standard contracts. The report argues that these changes had permitted greater access into the labour market for women and for lower-skilled workers. However, at the same time there is evidence that the increase in these forms of working conditions, often characterised as precarious, had an overall adverse effect on particular groups of people such as migrants, women, young and older workers and disabled workers and that it was closely associated with particular minority groups (McKay et al., 2012). The third driver, identified in the OECD report, was changes to working hours, which saw an increasing divide in hours worked between high- and low-waged workers. But it also needs to be borne in mind that low paid workers are more vulnerable to reductions in working hours than high-waged earners, contributing further to increases in income inequality (Anderson et al., 2006; Parutis, 2014). Finally, the fourth driver, according to the OECD, has been changes in tax and benefit systems that have resulted in less effective income redistribution. Changes in welfare systems across Europe have reduced access to benefits and this can also contribute to social inequalities, such that vulnerable groups fall into the risk of poverty (Beatty and Fothergill,

2013). Eurostat data for the period 2005 to 2010, on the efficiency of tax/ benefit systems in reducing poverty for women and men aged 18 to 64, shows that the tax/benefit system was unable to reduce poverty, especially for women (the EU27 average for men stood at 62% in 2005 and at 61% in 2010 and the equivalent for women was 57% in 2005 and 55% in 2010) and some countries, with well-established systems to prevent female poverty, for example Bulgaria, Denmark and Sweden, saw large increases (ETUI, 2012).

Economic Crisis and the Impact on Equality Policies

The economic crisis and the downturn have affected most aspects of society in the different Member States, for example growth prospects for Slovenia, Romania, Hungary and even Denmark are particularly poor; for the bailout countries, Greece and Portugal, the outcome of the economic downturn has been described as a humanitarian crisis; France, The Netherlands, Belgium, Germany, and Austria have succeeded in returning to pre-crisis production levels; and some Member States, such as Poland, Sweden and Slovakia have managed to achieve some economic growth (ETUI, 2012: 5). In most cases the economic crisis led to direct and indirect changes in labour law and in some Member States more acutely than others. For example Barnard (2012) suggests that reforms such as the Euro Plus Pact (EPP) of March 2011, the 'six pack' of Autumn of 2011 and the economic governance reports proposed by the Commission for the Eurozone in November 2011 are economic policies aimed at preventing Member States running large debts or at reducing debts but they also have a direct or indirect impact on labour law. For example in countries such as Greece, Ireland and Portugal which, as a result of the economic crisis, had required financial assistance from the Troika, their accompanying Memoranda of Understanding (MoU) gives a clear instruction for key reforms in labour law as a condition for receiving funds from the EU and the IMF and therefore enabling the deregulation of employment rights at national level, as a means of dealing the crisis. This model has also provided a framework for proposed changes to labour legislation in other Member States less affected by the crisis, for example the UK. Similarly, regarding collective dismissals, some Member States have either made changes to the consultation obligations of enterprises or adopted more flexible regulations (Muller, 2011). However the weakening of employment rights and employment protection, in some cases such as in the UK, Ireland or Germany, was already taking place prior to the crisis and became more incorporated into state policies as a result of an attempt to recover national economies (Heyes et al., 2012)

But what are the effects, if any, of the economic crisis on groups who tend to experience more disadvantages in the labour market, such as women, young people, older workers, the disabled, in fact all of the groups that we have identified in this study? This chapter therefore turns to consider the effects of the economic crisis on the equalities agenda within Europe, before then focusing on how trade unions have responded to the crisis in terms of their equality agendas.

A European Commission report on the impact of the economic crisis on men and women highlights the need for more equality measures, given that most Member States had not assessed their economic policies or the consolidation measures introduced, from a gender perspective (Bettio et al., 2013). The future of women's participation in the labour market, for example, could be challenging in a period of austerity, as the public sector which has been an important route for women's employment and career development has started to shrink. In addition diminishing public services may also result in women having to adopt the more 'traditional role' as unpaid carers (Rubery, 2013: 32)

Furthermore the 2012 Eurobarometer survey depicted a connection between discrimination and the economic downturn, showing that two-third of EU Member State citizens (67%) believed that older workers (those aged over 50) had experienced more discrimination as a result of the economic crisis. Over half of EU Member State citizens thought that discrimination had increased for disabled people (53%) and for people from different ethnic backgrounds (52%). Finally, 54% of EU Member State citizens (compared to 49% in the 2009 Eurobarometer survey) believed that equality and diversity policies were not considered as important because of the crisis and that they had received less funding as a result (Eurobarometer, 2012).[1] Using a more complex framework to study social inequalities (than had the OECD report discussed above), the 3rd European Quality of Life Survey (EQoL) also explored the impact of the economic crisis and found growing evidence of widening social inequalities between particular population groups (Eurofound, 2013). Using Amartya Sen's (1985, 1993) capabilities as a theoretical framework, which is defined as the freedom and opportunity a person has to live a life he or she chooses and values, the report identifies ten different capabilities: Life; Physical security; Legal security; Health; Education and learning; Standard of living; Productive and valued activities; Participation, influence, voice; Individual, family and social life; and Identity, expression, self-respect. The three aspects of inequality used by the EQoL survey include inequality of outcome, inequality in autonomy, and inequality in treatment. The study suggests that deprivation for women, older and younger people and disabled people had increased in the period between 2007 and 2011 and that this change could be attributed to the impacts of the economic crisis. For example women, older people and disabled people

---

1 http://ec.europa.eu/justice/newsroom/discrimination/news/121122_en.htm (accessed in June 2014).

had more difficulties in accessing health care; there was an increase of young people with mental health issues; and, in terms of standards of living, there was an increase in material deprivation for disabled people (and those with a limited disability) and for the long-term unemployed aged 50–64 (Eurofound, 2013). Furthermore the Eurofound (2012) 'Quality of life in Europe: impacts of crisis' report highlights that inequalities deepened as a result of the financial crisis leading to tensions especially between different racial and ethnic groups most notably in the Czech Republic, Hungary and Greece (Eurofound, 2012). The International Labour Organization (ILO), in a 2010 report, took a similar position, suggesting that the economic recession had a great impact on society and that not only had there been a decline in the index of life satisfaction, but that this decline was unprecedented (ILO report 2010).

Trade Union Equality Policies during the Economic Crisis

This section considers responses to the economic crisis and is based mainly on actions developed by the ETUC at European level, as the topic of economic crisis was not directly addressed by the Mapping study. Nevertheless as the research took place during the start of the economic crisis some respondents discussed their concerns on the societal impacts, especially in the area of race and ethnic relations. A main concern was that rising unemployment would increase hostility throughout Europe against migrant workers and ethnic minorities in general who were viewed in some cases as competitors for jobs and as outsiders in the society. This was also the view shared by many organisations across Europe and within the European Union. For example, on the 21st of March 2009 the Office for Democratic Institutions and Human Rights (ODIHR), the Council of Europe's European Commission against Racism and Intolerance (ECRI) and the European Union Agency for Fundamental Rights (FRA), to mark the occasion of the International Day for the Elimination of Racial Discrimination, issued a joined statement on the rise of intolerance towards migrants and minorities in Europe:

> Our organisations are alarmed by reports indicating an upsurge in violent attacks targeting migrants, refugees and asylum-seekers, and minorities such as the Roma. Europe's history demonstrates how economic depression can tragically lead to increasing social exclusion and persecution. We are concerned that in times of crisis, migrants, minorities and other vulnerable groups become 'scapegoats' for populist politicians and the media.[2]

---

2 http://fra.europa.eu/sites/default/files/fra_uploads/355-evt-21March-jointstatement-09_en.pdf (accessed in June 2014)

Trade union respondents discussed their concerns on the rising of xenophobia and racism inside and outside the workplace which can become more pronounced during a period of economic crisis. For example, a number of respondents to the Mapping study specifically identified a growth in anti-Roma attitudes, including both verbal and physical assault. An ETUCE project 'Developing non-discriminatory quality education for Roma children' between 2004 and 2006, aimed at tackling discrimination in education for Roma children, identified that a great majority of Roma children leave education before completing primary school. The ETCU programme (see also Chapter 4) was aimed at the inclusion of Roma children both in education and society and the programme worked with education systems, teachers and teacher trade unions to consider more effective methods of including them in education. The project focused on Bulgaria, Slovakia and Hungary, all three of which are Member States with large Roma populations (ETUCE, 2007: 4). The project helped provide training to increase teachers' capacity to teach multicultural classes and contributed to the establishment of national plans on Roma children and social exclusion.

Other trade union initiatives were developed to assist people from ethnic minority backgrounds into employment or career development. For example the Broadcasting, Entertainment, Cinematograph and Theatre Union (BECTU) in the UK had developed an initiative to help young ethnic minority workers into media careers by putting them into touch with media employers while the Netherlands Trade Union Confederation (FNV) launched a training initiative 'With all respect' which provided intensive training on diversity issues with the aim of bringing change to organisational cultures within the whole workforce, either on a one-to-one basis or through the existing works councils. Although these initiatives were not developed as a result of the economic crisis their work nevertheless was aimed at longer term outcomes taking account of the crisis.

Trade union officials in the Mapping study also discussed the position of migrant workers in the labour market, who may become more precarious as a result of the crisis, with worsening working conditions, acceptance of lower wages or overall poorer conditions and cuts in social protection and benefits, in order to keep their jobs. There may also be incentives to overstay and to work with irregular status (ILO, 2011). Migrant workers may be faced with the prospect of losing their jobs as a result of social prejudices and stereotyping which increases in periods of crisis. The OECD International Migration Outlook 2013 report highlights that unemployment rates for foreign born workers in the OECD countries has risen by five percentage points in the period between 2008 and 2012, compared with three percentage points for the native-born (OECD, 2013: 11). The same report also argues that the prospects of finding a job for long term unemployed migrants and their children are limited and although it is difficult to measure discrimination, studies have shown that migrants and the children of migrants have to submit twice as many job applications than people with no migration background and equivalent CV in order to secure an interview or a job (OECD, 2013: 12).

In general the economic crisis produced a varied reaction amongst trade union respondents in the Mapping study. In terms of membership, trade union respondents expressed opposing views on the effects of the economic crisis on their membership levels. Some described a decline or a potential drop in their membership, as members were expected to lose their jobs. Others, however, argued that even in the middle of an economic crisis there were opportunities to recruit new members. More specifically, on the issue of equality and anti-discrimination, even among those who had demonstrated a genuine commitment to pursuing a union agenda on equality and diversity, some were clearly unsure as to whether they would be in a position to continue their activities to the standards that they wished, as, in a period of deep crisis, when unions need to deal with multiple problems, equality issues risked being relegated. Some trade union participants appeared committed to continuing their initiatives in relation to the protection of disadvantaged groups and to promoting equality agendas and equal and fair treatment which in itself can be a response and a challenge to the economic crisis and its rationale. The following two initiatives from Romania and Lithuania, which formed the basis for two case studies in the Mapping study, illustrate this viewpoint.

Case study example F

Example 1: older workers in rural areas

The Democratic Trade Union Confederation of Romania (Confederaţia Sindicatelor Democratice – CSDR) represents both the public sector and the private sector and is affiliated to ETUC (European Trade Union Confederation). The union developed an initiative 'The TIC caravan' which was introduced by the Postgraduate Institute Phoenix, in partnership with the Transylvanian Plains Inter-Municipal Cooperation and equality experts from the CSDR, with the aim of reducing the level of reticence of older workers, especially older women living and working in rural areas mainly in the sector of agriculture, seeking training and retraining. This initiative was similar to earlier trade union policies aimed at promoting the labour rights of women in general and older workers in particular.

Economic and socio-political events in the country had influenced the development of this scheme, including large-scale redundancies as a result of the process of restructuring, reorganisation and privatisation;

---

the establishment of the tripartite social and economic council (CES) and the National Commission for Equal Opportunities; and the law on unemployment insurance and the stimulation of employment.

The initiative tried to secure the participation of older workers in the professional conversion and career development programmes that were on offer but one of the difficulties was the often low self-esteem combined with the long working hours of agriculture workers. To overcome these difficulties, and to increase participation, a partnership was formed with the local government, the local inter-municipal association and civil society organisations who worked in small groups but targeted 250 women in rural areas. A CSDR equality representative coordinated the job search and the training and career counselling sessions, which familiarised the participants with their employment rights and with the equal opportunities legislation.

The partnership formed for this initiative and the cooperation of the social actors, local government, trade union and civil society organisations contributed to a better understanding of local skills and resources and helped introduce adult learning services into Romanian rural areas. By 31 August 2009 around 63 people had participated in the training for job search and 62 in the careers' counselling. Of these the majority (86 %) were women. The positive impact of the initiative had led to a consideration for spreading the programme to other rural areas while engaging with other partners in developing programmes for young people and adults and for the labour market integration of people belonging to the Roma minority. The programme also included a focus on the development of skills beyond the labour market; familiarisation with labour rights and national anti-discrimination legislation, as well as with the institutional structures aimed at protecting labour rights.

Example 2: reintegration of older workers in the labour market

The Lithuanian Trade Union Confederation (LPSK) is a member of International Trade Union Confederation (ITUC), and the European Trade Union Confederation (ETUC). In 2005 LPSK, in partnership with other regional and international bodies such as NGOs, equality bodies and educational establishments developed a project for the protection of older workers in the labour market called 'Support network for reintegration into the labour market in the region of Utena and Vilnius'. The project was aimed at identifying and drawing the attention of government officials, employers and wider society to the problems faced by older people within the national labour market and developed a plan to eliminate them. The project was funded partly by the European Social Fund and partly by the Republic of Lithuania and it was carried out within the EQUAL programme framework in the period between 2005 and 2008.

The initiative was developed within a national context where age discrimination was described to the Mapping study as common place and widespread but that its impact was subtle and difficult to substantiate. The main reason for that was the rapid social and economic changes that had taken place in Lithuania within the last years, increasing demand for a new highly qualified labour force. Older people who had gained their skills and qualifications during the Soviet period had not been successful in adapting to a changed environment of new technologies and a highly competitive labour environment. As a consequence there is high and long term unemployment for this group of people.

As part of the project the LPSK Education Support unit carried out research on age discrimination and the reasons for inequality in the two regions. More than 40% of the people participating in this research reported that they experienced discrimination because of their age and 82% claimed that their employer never offered them retraining opportunities. The research and the broader aim of the initiative concentrated on providing possibilities for reintegrating older people in the labour market, provided training and re-qualification schemes and campaigned to raise awareness on issues of age discrimination and the problems that older workers might encounter at work. One awareness-raising activity included a radio programme called 'From salary to salary' and was broadcast on the First Programme of the National Radio in Lithuania. The impact of the programme, apart from raising awareness to a wider public, also motivated and recruited older people to join the initiative. The outcome of this initiative was a set of recommendations to the Tripartite Council in 2008 which were accepted and implemented into collective agreements and brought into the Labour Code of the Republic of Lithuania. The recommendations included policies for job protection for those near retirement age and paid time-off for retraining, particularly for workers that were under the threat of redundancy. In addition a new support network was created consisting of trade unions, public organisations and vocational schools. In total 352 older workers, among them 74 unemployed, took part in the training provided by the project and 52 found new employment while four older workers were promoted to directors and chief executives. What was more important was that the project reported continuous activity even after its completion, as the needs of older workers had become part of the trade union agendas and were discussed if appropriate at the Tripartite Council.

Although the two initiatives took place either before or at the start of the economic crisis, they were developed in countries that had experienced a rapid socio-economic crisis. What both examples show is that equality and diversity issues remain just as relevant and important and can still be tackled in times of economic crisis. What the two case studies have in common is the successful completion of the initiatives through partnerships, their development within a national context where there might have been a low awareness of equality and antidiscrimination issues and within of a framework of economic and social crisis. Both projects by focusing on the human costs of the economic crisis aimed at and, to a certain degree, were successful in mainstreaming age discrimination and introducing policies that challenged existing structures.

The ETUC Manifesto on the European Parliament Elections 2014 opposed the current austerity policies and stated that cohesion, social justice and equality needed to be reinforced and that equally racism, xenophobia, homophobia, nationalism and extremism need to be combated rigorously.[3] Since the start of the economic crisis debates on migration in Europe have intensified and policies over border controls and controls over the mobility of third country citizens have strengthened and 'fortress Europe' is a term often used to describe these new policies of tightening migration (Kofman and Sales, 1992). Workers' mobility and the rights of migrants have been an integral part of trade union policies at national and European level and the ETUC Strategy Action Plan (2011–2015)[4] explicitly makes the point that these groups need protecting in this period of economic downturn during which we are witnessing 'the rise of populism and xenophobic political parties in an increasing number of EU countries where the scapegoats are migrants from both within and outside the EU' (2011: 59).

The Mapping study found that the largest number of initiatives (52 out of 130) developed by trade unions in the 34 countries were focused on discrimination based on race and ethnicity and that many were aimed at strengthening the rights of migrant workers. The General Confederation of Portuguese Workers (CGTP) had negotiated an agreement for cleaning workers that allowed migrants in manufacturing to accumulate two months of their holiday to travel back to their home countries and the initiative of the Commercial Workers Union – Handels (Sweden) local section to establish a centre for undocumented workers are just two of the many examples mentioned in the research. A look at some of the ETUC work during the period of the economic crisis shows that trade unions continued their work in supporting migrant workers. In 2009 the ETUC acknowledged two important changes that

---

3 http://www.etuc.org/documents/etuc-manifesto-european-parliament-elections#.U3sWnHZLqP8 (accessed May 2014).

4 http://www.etuc.org/etuc-strategy-and-action-plan-2011–2015–0 (accessed May 2014).

had occurred, namely the entrance of Romania and Bulgaria to the EU and the international economic crisis which had affected the EU. As a consequence the ETUC passed a 'Resolution on conditions for free movement: more protection of workers and fair competition' stressing the need for proper consultation with the social partners on freedom of movement, combining open borders with adequate protection for workers. These, according to the ETUC, had been undermined by the rise of precarious jobs and outsourcing; insufficient measures to tackle the crisis in many countries; the border mobility of workers (via subcontractors and intermediaries) leading to unfair competition on wages and working conditions; as well as, in relation to those cases where migrant workers were employed as undeclared workers and as (false) self-employed.[5] A year later, in 2010, the ETUC called for a Social Progress Protocol to be included in the Treaties so that fundamental social rights could take priority and for a series of revisions to the Directive on posted workers, with legislation that might eliminate unfair competition and promote equal treatment for different groups of workers.[6] In 2013 the ETUC promoted an action plan for a policy on migration, for the 2014–2018 period of the DG Home Affairs and EU2020 strategy, to strengthen legislation for the protection of migrant workers.[7] More recently, and focusing on the issue of equality all workers, the ETUC urged MEPs in 2014 to vote for the rights to the equal treatment of workers in the same workplace under the Intra-Corporate Transfer' Directive (ICT Directive) in order to secure equal work conditions for all and, according to Luca Visentini, Confederal Secretary of the ETUC:

> The ETUC is strongly in favour of more and more transparent ways of letting in workers from outside the EU. But migrant workers must be treated exactly the same as locals in the same workplace. Bumping up shareholder profits by importing cheaper workers is totally unacceptable to European citizens and taxpayers.[8]

The labour market in recent years has been experiencing another period of change with a rise in non-standard and atypical forms of employment, the growth of both voluntary and involuntary part-time work, and of temporary

---

5 http://www.etuc.org/documents/etuc-resolution-conditions-free-movement-more-protection-workers-and-fair-competition#.U3r4hHZLqP8 (accessed May 2014).

6 http://www.etuc.org/documents/resolution-equal-treatment-and-non-discrimination-migrant-workers#.U3r5XHZLqP8 (accessed May 2014).

7 http://www.etuc.org/documents/action-plan-migration#.U3r1jnZLqP8 (accessed May 2014).

8 http://www.etuc.org/press/meps-urged-vote-equal-treatment-workers#.U80ak0CTEvI (accessed May 2014).

contracts, alongside reforms designed to provide flexibility to employers permitting the more ready hiring and dismissing of workers. At the same time the workforce itself has become more heterogeneous in Europe, with for example, a greater participation of women or of migrant workers from different ethnic and religious backgrounds in the European labour market, or as a result of policies which facilitate the entry of disabled people into the workplace, or gay and lesbian people becoming more open about their sexuality in the workplace. Such changes in the workforce also reflect the general demographic changes and trends in society as a whole and according to Gumbrell-Mccormick and Hyman (2013: 34) there is a common argument in many European states that claims that these changes can pose a challenge to trade unions whose 'traditional working-class values of collectivism have given way to more individualistic orientations'. The authors however acknowledge that this view may be over-simplistic. Attracting young people into trade union membership for example can be challenging, as trade unions in EU countries report lower membership among young workers than among other groups (Eurofound, 2012a) often attributed to lack of interest although it is probably true to say that historically the trade union movement has always been more likely to represent older, than younger, workers. Research has shown that younger people are more likely to work under precarious conditions and often in unorganised workplaces where unions have limited access as well as that young people have been particularly affected by high unemployment rates resulting in a prolonged absence from the labour market (Kretsos, 2011). In periods of economic crisis workers in atypical forms of employment can be considered as more distant from the trade unions, as one trade union interviewee noted:

> those workers are more distant from the unions because they are afraid. It is more difficult to inform them about their rights, because they are temporary workers and they face much more pressure in the workplace than the permanent workers (Portugal, trade union official).

Furthermore the Eurofound (2012a: 14) report highlights that trade unions in different countries have an awareness of the position of young people in the labour market, especially as a consequence of the economic crisis, and that they have developed initiatives to actively encourage membership from young people and that they continue in their efforts to recruit young workers; they lobby for the promotion of more extensive use of apprenticeships and training in order to integrate young workers as well as promoting the reform of education systems; and in addition they campaign to improve progress from education to the labour market and to increase more job opportunities for young workers. The European Union had also decided to designate 2012 as the European Year for Active Ageing and Solidarity between Generations (EY 2012) which further raised awareness of the problems that younger or older workers experience in periods of economic crisis.[9] In 2013 the ETUC through the collaboration of its Youth Committee and the European Federation of Retired and Older People (FERPA) (both affiliated to the ETUC) expressed a commitment to the principles contained in the EY 2012. In 2013 the ETUC developed an Active Ageing Agenda focusing on intergenerational solidarity by enabling young people to enter the labour market at the same time as older workers remained in employment, aiming first to guarantee the highest quality jobs and second to guarantee a high quality of life. The ETUC was of the view that these could be materialised through action at legislative level, by improving working and living conditions and by making education and training systems more effective.[10]

Gender inequality and discrimination is another area where trade unions have continued their equality and anti-discrimination work in a context where research has shown that the economic crisis can have a negative impact on gender equality. A study on 'Gender Equality, Employment Policies and the Crisis in EU Member States' (Villa and Smith, 2010) found that the impact of the crisis, from a gender perspective, has been similar to that in previous crises, that is men have been affected first, as they are concentrated in the trade sectors, whereas women's employment falls when demand in consumer services falls and when public sector cuts are being made. The authors found that what was different this time round was that because women have had a greater share in employment in recent years they were also hit in the first wave of the crisis (Villa and Smith, 2010). At a policy level the authors also found that gender mainstreaming has not had as much of a priority as 'neither the European Economic Recovery Plan nor the subsequent Prague Summit made a mention of "gender", "women" or "equality"' (Villa and Smith, 2010: 7). Similarly, Leschke and Jepsen (2011) in their comparative study of Denmark, Germany and the UK observed that the cuts in social security systems, as a result of the austerity measures, affected women more than men and they emphasised the need for more gender assessment methods in government policies in order to preserve equality. The Mapping study did not directly analyse gender-specific initiatives, as its main aim was to concentrate on the other grounds protected by the Employment Directive 2000/78, however, some of the initiatives analysed, particularly in relation to LGBT issues did have a gender element. Overall the work of trade unions, at European level, shows that the relationship between the economic crisis and potential gender discrimination has been of concern to the trade unions. More specifically, in the area of gender, the ETUC Strategy

---

9 www.etuc.org/ ... /etuc-action-plan-active-ageing-and-solidarity (accessed in May 2014).

10 http://www.etuc.org/documents/etuc-action-plan-active-ageing-and-solidarity-between-generations#.U3uB_HZLqP8 (accessed in May 2014).

Action Plan highlighted that the unequal distribution of unpaid work between men and women inhibited gender equality, while policies on work, family and private life were being mistakenly conceived as a matter for women rather than for both parents (ETUC, 2011: 21).[11]

In 2012 the ETUC adopted an Action Programme on Gender Equality with which it committed itself to pursue its objectives on gender mainstreaming in all ETUC policies and actions, to achieve equal pay, to eliminate the gender representation gap in decision-making bodies, to promote the combination of work, family and private life and to address the link between domestic violence and workplace rights.[12] Continuing its 'ETUC 8th of March surveys', in March 2014 ETUI conducted a survey of 51 (out of 85) national confederations from 31 European countries, first to assess the progress that had been made in reducing the representation gap between women and men and to highlight successful gender mainstreaming activities within affiliated organisations, and second to explore trade union strategies to address violence against women (Bouaffre and Sechi, 2014).[13] The survey found that female membership across the participating trade union confederations was at 44.2%, a slight increase from the previous year (43.4% in 2013). However in terms of positions of power within national confederations, women were in a minority compared to men (four female Presidents as against 35 male; 18 female Vice-Presidents as against 51 male; nine female General Secretaries as against 27 male; seven female Deputy General Secretaries as against 13 male; and nine female treasurers as against 16 male).

In terms of violence against women, the same survey found that a large number of unions in Europe had developed some form of action to address the issue, ranging from campaigning to awareness-raising events and conducting surveys. The report highlighted that more work was needed in bringing these issues into collective bargaining agreements as only a few had incorporated the specific issue of violence against women. Although the above survey did not directly address the issue of economic crisis it can be assumed that, as data was collected a period of austerity, it is also reflective of the time it was taken. Moreover concerns for the future of gender equality were raised by respondents of the ETUC survey from countries hard hit by the recession. In particular the GSEE (Greece) respondent to the ETUC survey reported that the economic crisis and the austerity measures had ignored the issue of gender equality and for women victims of violence this was a particular problem as in

---

11 http://www.etuc.org/etuc-strategy-and-action-plan-2011–2015–0 (accessed May 2014).

12 http://www.etuc.org/documents/etuc-action-programme-gender-equality#. U3tDGXZLqP8 (accessed May 2014).

13 http://www.etuc.org/sites/www.etuc.org/files/other/files/etuc_8th_march_ survey_2014_en_0.pdf (accessed May 2014).

many European countries including Greece there was a lack of shelters that offered protection for abused women and there was also a lack of effective access to justice.

Apart from gender, the ETUC Strategy and Action Plan (2011–2015), adopted by its last Congress in 2011, underlined the need for continuous action to promote equality:

> Equality is an essential goal of trade union action. It is a principle enshrined in the Treaty and in various Directives which address equality between men and women and the fight against all forms of discrimination on grounds of gender, belief, race, age, disability, sexual orientation, nationality, economic status, ill health, or any other form. Inequality in our societies and on the labour market is far from having been eliminated (ETUC, 2011: 50).

In the area of anti-discrimination action, in 2010 ETUC had expressed solidarity with LGBT workers on the International Day against Homophobia and Transphobia, as research had shown that prejudice, harassment and violence were still experienced by LGBT people at their workplaces.[14] Moreover the rise of the extreme political right, often as a response to the economic crisis, had contributed to increased homophobia in various parts of Europe such as in Greece (Vaiou, 2014), France (Waters, 2013) and Italy (Botti and D'Ippoliti, 2014). The EU LGBT survey by the Fundamental Rights Agency (FRA) found that around 47% of the respondents had personally experienced discrimination and harassment on the grounds of sexual orientation (FRA, 2013) and lesbian women in the youngest age group, between 18 and 24 years old, and those with the lowest incomes, were most likely to report discrimination in the last 12 months. Beyond the workplace one in three respondents had reported discrimination on one or more grounds including seeking accommodation, accessing healthcare, attending school or university, themselves or as a parent, or in accessing services, such as restaurants, nightclubs, banks or insurance or in visits to clubs (FRA, 2013: 17). Tackling discrimination against the LGBT community has also taken the form of a joint action between trade unions and NGOs; for example, in 2012, the ETUC announced a commitment to work jointly with the ETUCE and ILGA-Europe towards the elimination of bullying and discrimination on the basis of sexual orientation, gender identity and gender expression within schools.[15]

---

14 http://www.etuc.org/press/etuc-expresses-solidarity-lgbt-workers-international-day-against-homophobia-and-transphobia#.U3twxHZLqP8 (accessed May 2014).

15 http://www.etuc.org/press/etuc-etuce-and-ilga-europe-commit-work-jointly-combat-homophobic-bullying-schools-workplaces#.U3t2M3ZLqP8 (accessed May 2014).

Studies have indicated that the consequences of economic crisis have had an effect on the physical and mental health of the population. Karanikolos et al. (2013), using data from the EU-SILC survey, and covering the years 2006–2008 and 2008–2010, carried out a comparative study aiming at finding out whether unhealthy persons were more likely to lose their jobs in a period of economic crisis and whether a higher level of protection might lessen the impact. This comparative research found that ill health increases the risk of job loss; however the gap between disabled and non-disabled people had narrowed during the period of economic crisis, mainly due to the accelerated job losses of non-disabled people. The study also found that stronger employment measures provided protection for disabled people but this link was less clear during times of economic crisis. But in terms of mental health, an ILO report states that it is policy choices that determine whether the economic recession will have an impact on mental health outcomes, as recent data suggests that active labour market programmes aimed at helping people to retain their jobs or that provide family support measures or access to mental health services have been effective in preventing the worsening of mental health as a result of the economic crisis (ILO, 2011: 8). In 2011, the ETUC together with the European Disability Forum (EDF) put emphasis on the need for appropriate policies and actions that would permit the labour market to become more inclusive, especially during the period of financial crisis with the reduction of social budgets, job insecurity and the rise of unemployment[16] As the ETUC Strategy and Action Plan (2011–2015) suggests, dependency relating to age or disability will require the provision of affordable and high quality care services in order to allow people concerned and their families to live with dignity.

Conclusion

This chapter has attempted to plot the directions taken by trade unions in relation to their equality agendas in a period of economic crisis. Studies have shown that there are increasing income disparities and wage gaps between rich and poor, fuelling social inequality and poverty within European Member States. At the time of writing there has been a continuing and sustained economic and political upheaval in many areas of Europe, with strong anti-immigration agendas and criticisms over the role and function of the European Union. In this context it is clear that trade union equality policies face new challenges which some organisations have found the tools to respond to, thus continuing to pursue their equality aims, whereas others have not. We would

16 http://www.etuc.org/press/trade-unions-and-disability-movement-together-more-inclusive-labour-market#.U3ubdXZLqP8 (accessed in May 2014).

suggest, however, that the responses that trade unions present in times of crisis might also reflect the overall extent of their support for equality issues. In other words, those unions with weak commitments to equality were more likely to cite the economic crisis as a reason for inactivity or for the ceasing of activity, whereas those with stronger commitments to equality were more likely to find arguments within the crisis itself as to why it would be necessary to continue with their existing policy agendas.

Chapter 9
Conclusion – Looking to the Future

In this concluding chapter we move to reflect on the potential wider role of trade unions in promoting equality at work and to challenging those accounts that suggest that economic crisis must inevitably lead to a downgrading of these issues. This is not to accept that there have been, and will continue to be, challenges to trade unions in advancing the claim for equality at work and in wider society, but at their core these challenges are not new. As we have demonstrated in previous chapters, where trade unions are reticent about pursuing equality, the reasons are to be found more in their own politics, in an unwillingness to confront the status quo, and in a trade union membership that has not been sufficiently informed so as to recognise the benefits of equality to all workers, rather than in an external economic situation that would make them divert from a focus on equality. Thus where trade unions suggest that it is the historic situation that is holding them back from defending the right to equal treatment, such claims must be questioned. Trade unions that are active proponents of equality remain so, regardless of whether its achievement appears more difficult or not.

In our analysis of the equality directives in Chapter 3 we argued that legislation itself has been insufficient to eliminate discrimination and that this was one reason why it was necessary to explore the role of trade unions in this field. We know that across Europe as a whole few claims are taken to the tribunals and courts that rely on the provisions of the directives and, furthermore, that Europe's citizens generally are not knowledgeable as to what rights they have under EU law. We also reflect on whether, despite the introduction of the EU directives, workers now experience a more unequal society than they did before the economic crisis. The rise in unemployment, particularly among specific groups like younger and older workers, migrant and minority ethnic workers and women, inevitably reduces their access to equality. At the same time, as Wilkinson and Pickett (2009) have demonstrated, societies that are more unequal are also more dysfunctional. In relation to the impact of the economic crisis they note:

> We live in a pessimistic period. As well as being worried by the likely consequences of global warming, it is easy to feel that many societies are, despite their material success, increasingly burdened by their social failings, and now, as if to add to our woes, we have the economic recession and its aftermath of high unemployment (2009: ix).

If the economic crisis has indeed limited the movement forward for equality, simply because business reflects on other imperatives than promoting equality, and as a consequence the gap between those with abundant resources and those with none or few widens, then society itself at all levels is damaged, according to the detailed data which Wilkinson and Pickett (2009) have drawn on. Thus the challenge to inequality is not just about assisting those at the bottom to move up, it is about making our societies more equal and therefore functional. Discrimination is bad for a wider group than just those who have experienced it.

We have stated that it is important to identify who the key actors are that might be positioned to challenge inequality. We have concluded that, despite the weakening of their collective bargaining power in many Member States, the trade union movement at national and European level, however imperfect, remains the most effective actor in relation to challenging workplace discrimination. However, both the impact of the economic crisis itself and the fact that equality cannot be addressed exclusively within the workplace, is the reason why actions are likely to be more effective where they are built through alliances between trade unions and other civil society actors. The inability of the law, of itself, to eliminate discrimination at work is why trade unions can play a pivotal role but we also note that they are not always positioned to do this by themselves and this is why we have highlighted the advantages of collaborative work between trade unions and non-governmental organisations. In a context where trade union influence throughout Europe is weaker than it was in the post war period through to the 1970s, it is the combined power of trade unions in the workplace and NGOs with their links to wider society and in particular their focus on specific grounds of discrimination, that can challenge discriminatory treatment. Additionally, as we have demonstrated, the EU directives recognise the role of the trade unions in challenging discrimination and afford them representational rights where Member States are accepting of such a role. Unfortunately in some countries, and particularly in the UK, governments have been hostile to the notion of providing trade unions with a specific representational role. To adhere to this trade unions and NGOs have needed to learn to work in new ways. This has often been difficult for both types of organisation and in Chapter 6 we have referred to the tensions that do exist between them due to different ways of working, different constituencies and responsibilities. But organisations can learn to work in new ways and the collaboration of trade unions and NGOs has resulted in their bringing different communities together. In doing this they provide adherents of both organisations with the opportunity to think and to act in new ways and the examples cited of trade union organisation with LGBT bodies demonstrate the advantages of such collaboration. Working collaboratively may also offer workers a method of better resisting any attempts by management to discontinue non-discrimination policies. Particularly in times of crisis trade unions working with other civil society organisations can be the voice of the oppressed.

One of the themes developed in this book has been around the concept of 'hard' and 'soft' issues in relation to the non-discrimination strands. We have shown that where trade unions act as single organisations then they are more likely to address only 'soft' issues, such as those around gender or disability, where there is more likely to be a general consensus of these being issues that merit trade union involvement. It is around what we have termed as 'hard' issues – the non-discrimination strands around ethnicity, sexual orientation and discrimination against Roma peoples, in particular – where trade unions appear to operate more effectively where they are in partnership, either with trade union sister organisations in other Member States, with European level trade union organisations or with other civil society organisations like NGOs. We have also argued that the absence of an organisational structural base to deal with non-discrimination displays both advantages and disadvantages. Unlike the situation in areas where there is a legal structure (for example with EWCs) the fact that the parties are not constrained by having to operate within specific structures may free them to adopt different strategies and policies that suit particular situations and times.

Nevertheless, this focus has also served to highlight the weaknesses which are also present in the trade union responses. In particular, the role of funding in the promotion of equality measures has meant that the directions that trade unions and other civil society organisations take, the issues that they campaign on, the discrimination that they work to counter, is directed by the funding itself. The absence of funding thus means also the absence of activity and of policy. Trade unions are therefore more likely to take up those issues that they know will be supported financially by government and at EU level. The risk is that policy makers can use this propensity to organise around issues that are funded, to determine which areas of discrimination should be combatted. There is another risk, not just that of pushing trade unions in the direction of where there is funding, but that it also legitimises some areas of activity as opposed to others. We saw this in relation in particular to cross border and European level trade union initiatives, as although the data suggests that this is the level through which national trade unions will take up new issues, it also risks delivering messages that some areas of equality should take precedence over others. This is not the same as saying that all forms of inequality are the same, as some forms are particularly destructive to society, but in legitimising some non-discrimination activities there is always the risk that others consequently appear de-legitimised.

If the core arguments are that inequality should be combatted and that collaboration brings additional advantages then it is important to identify those factors that promoted equality and collaboration. The data collected in the

Mapping study suggests that bringing organisations together is effective. It also suggests that external factors like migration can act as a catalyst to extending trade union influence beyond the narrow confines of the workplace. Finally it must be recognised that discrimination is multi-layered and that here trade unions seem less well placed to respond. As we noted in Chapter 7 there has been little trade union activity around the issue of multiple discrimination. There is a lack of understanding as to what it means and how it can be addressed. There is still a focus on the individual strands of discrimination and of course it may be that it is the very collaboration that we have witnessed between trade unions and NGOs that has made it more difficult for trade unions to consider the multiple facets of discrimination as NGOs are built around the specifics of strand discrimination. Thus in conclusion we might also posit that while these collaborations have brought trade unions to new ways of thinking and acting, they may also limit them from looking beyond the strand and into the complexity of multiple discrimination.

Trade unions remain one of the largest membership organisations in Europe. However, as Fanelli and Brogan argue 'If trade unions and working class communities are to resist austerity, rebuilding the capacities of organized labour to fight back against concessionary demands must seek to build community-labour coalitions from the bottom up'. Furthermore they assert that if unions want to assert their potential as transformative organisations 'they will need to be reinvented' which requires that they 'move beyond the limited defence of their own members' interests and fight for the interests of the working class as a whole' (2014: 116). In this book we have at least suggested that this is a direction that many trade unions in Europe are now beginning to explore. It may be too early to assert that this will have been effective in reversing the decline in workers' power and in establishing a general right to equality, but it does show that there are options which are now being explored that could have a significant impact on the direction of trade unions in the coming period.

Bibliography

Abrams, K. (1994), 'Title VII and the complex female subject', *Michigan Law Review*, 92(8), pp. 2479–2540

Age Platform Europe (2013), *AGE contribution to the European Commission's assessment of the transposition and application of the Employment Equality Directive (2000/78/EC)*, Age Platform Europe

Ahmet, A.M., Andersson, L., and Hammarstedt, M. (2013), 'Are gay men and lesbians discriminated against in the hiring process?' *Southern Economic Journal*, 79(3), pp. 565–585

Alberti, G., Holgate, J., and Tapia, M. (2013), 'Organising migrants as workers or as migrant workers? Intersectionality, trade unions and precarious work', *The International Journal of Human Resource Management*, 24(22), pp. 4132–4148

Amnesty International (2013), *Submission to the European Commission on the implementation of the equality directives*, Amnesty International

Anner, M., and P. Evans (2004), 'Building Bridges Across a Double Divide: Alliances Between US and Latin American Labour and NGOs', *Development in Practice*, 14(1–2), pp. 34–47

Anner, M., Greer, I., Hauptmeier, M., Lillie, N., and Winchester, N. (2006), 'The industrial determinants of transnational solidarity: global inter-union politics in three sectors', *European Journal of Industrial Relations*, 12(1), pp. 7–27

Anthias, F., and Yuval-Davis, N. (1983) 'Contextualising Feminism: Gender, Ethnic and Class Divisions', *Feminist Review*, 15, pp. 62–75

Anthias, F., and Yuval-Davis, N. (1992), *Racialised Boundaries. Race, Nation, Gender, Colour and Class*. London: Routledge

Archer, L. (2007), 'Diversity, equality and higher education: a critical reflection on the ab/uses of equity discourse within widening participation', *Teaching in Higher Education*, 12(5–6), pp. 635–653

Arenas, D., Lozano, J.M., and Albareda, L. (2009), 'The Role of NGOs in CSR: Mutual Perceptions Among Stakeholders', *Journal of Business Ethics*, 88(1), pp. 175–197

Baker, J., Lynch, K., Cantillon, S., and Walsh, J. (2009), *Equality: From Theory to Action*, 2nd edition. Basingstoke: Palgrave Macmillan

Barnard (2012), 'The Financial Crisis and the Euro Plus Pact: A Labour Lawyer's Perspective', *Industrial Law Journal*, 41(1), pp. 98–114

Bernaciak, M. (2010) 'Cross-border competition and trade union responses in the enlarged EU: Evidence from the automotive industry in Germany and Poland', *European Journal of Industrial Relations*, 16(2), pp. 119–135

Bernaciak, M. (2010), 'Cross-border competition and trade union responses in the enlarged EU: Evidence from the automotive industry in Germany and Poland', *European Journal of Industrial Relations*, 16(2), pp. 119–135

Bettio, F., Corsi, M., Lyberaki, A., Samek Lodovici, M. and Verashchagina, A. (2013), *The impact of the economic crisis on the situation of women and men and on gender equality policies (3MB PDF), Synthesis report*, Publications Office of the European Union, Luxembourg

Botti, F., and D'Ippoliti, C. (2014), 'Don't ask don't tell (that you're poor). Sexual orientation and social exclusion in Italy', *Journal of Behavioural and Experimental Economics*, 49, pp. 8–25

Bouaffre A., and Sechi, S. (2014), *ETUC 8th March Survey 2014, 7th edition*, European Trade Union Institute

Bradley, H. (1996), *Fractured Identities*. Cambridge: Polity Press

Bradley, H. (1989), *Men's work, women's work*. Cambridge: Polity Press

Brah, A. (1996), *Cartographies of Diaspora: Contesting Identities*. London: Routledge

Bratton, M. (1989), 'The politics of NGO–government relations in Africa', *World Development*, 17(4), pp. 569–587

Braun, R., and Gearhart, J. (2004), 'Who should code your conduct? Trade union and NGO differences in the fight for workers' rights', *Development in Practice*, 14(1–2), pp. 183–196

Brown, W., and Marsden, D. (2010), *Individualisation and the Growing Diversity of Employment Relationships*. London: Centre for Economic Performance, London School of Economics

Brown, W., Deakin, S., Nash, D. and Oxenbridge, S. (2000), 'The employment contract: From collective procedures to individual rights', *British Journal of Industrial Relations*, 38(4), pp. 611–629

Burri, S. and Schiek, D. (2009), *Multiple Discrimination in EU Law Opportunities for Legal Responses to Intersectional Gender Discrimination?* European Network of Legal Experts in the Field of Gender Equality, European Commission Directorate-General for Employment, Social Affairs and Equal Opportunities

Charnovitz, S. (1997), 'Two centuries of participation: NGOs and international governance', *Michigan Journal of International Law*, 18(2), 183–286

Chopin, I. and Uyen Do, T. (2012), *Developing anti-discrimination law in Europe*, European Commission, Directorate General for Justice

Chun, J. (2013), 'Organizing workers at the margins: new strategies and organizational forms for immigrant and women workers employed in low-paid, precarious jobs', *Internationale Solidarität Revisited – Gewerkschaften im Spiegel globaler Migrationsprozesse*, Heinrich-Böll-Stiftung

Cisar, O. and Vrablikova, K. (2013), 'Transnational activism of social movement organizations: The effect of European Union funding on local groups in the Czech Republic', *European Union Politics*, 14(1), pp. 140–160

Cockburn, C. (1995), 'Women's Access to European Industrial Relations', *European Journal of Industrial Relations*, 1(171)

Colgan, F., Wright, T., Creegan, C. and McKearney, A. (2006), 'Lesbian, Gay and Bisexual Workers, Equality, Diversity and Inclusion in the Workplace', *Equal Opportunities International, Professional Insights*, 25(6), pp. 465–470

Colling, T., (2006), 'What space for unions on the floor of rights? Trade unions and the enforcement of statutory individual employment rights', *Industrial Law Journal*, 35(2), pp. 140–160

Collins, P.H. (2000), 'It's All in the Family: Intersections of Gender, Race, and Nation', in U. Narayan and S. Harding (eds), *Decentering the Center: Philosophy for a Multicultural, Postcolonial, and Feminist World*. Bloomington: Indiana University Press, pp. 156–176

Combahee River Collective (1982), 'A Black Feminist Statement', in: *All the Women Are White, All the Blacks Are Men, But Some of Us are Brave: Black Women's Studies*. New York: Feminist Press, pp. 13–22

Commission of the European Communities (2005), *Communication from the Commission to the Council, the European, Parliament, the European Economic and Social Committee and the Committee of the Regions. "Non-Discrimination and Equal Opportunities for All – a Framework Strategy"*, available at: http://www.europarl.europa.eu/registre/docs_autres_institutions/commission_europeenne/com/2005/0224/COM_COM%282005%290224_EN.pdf (accessed June 2014)

Compa, L. (2004), 'Trade unions, NGOs, and corporate codes of conduct', *Development in Practice*, 14(1–2), pp. 210–221

Crenshaw, K. (1989), 'Demarginalizing the intersection of Race and Sex: A Black Feminist Critique of Antidiscrimination Doctrine, Feminist Theory and Antiracist Politics', in: *University of Chicago Legal Forum 1989*, pp. 137–167

Crenshaw, K. (1991), 'Mapping the Margins: Intersectionality, Identity Politics, and Violence against Women of Color', *Stanford Law Review*, 43(6), pp. 1241–1299

Crenshaw, K. (1992), 'Whose Story Is It, Anyway? Feminist and Antiracist Appropriations of Anita Hill', in: Morrison, T. (ed.), *Race-ing, Justice, En-gendering Power*. New York: Pantheon Books, pp. 402–440

Curran, D. and Quinn, M. (2012), 'Attitudes to employment law and the consequent impact of legislation on employment relations practice', *Employee Relations*, 34(5), pp. 464–480

Davies, B. (2003), 'Death to Critique and Dissent? The Policies and Practices of New Managerialism and of Evidence-based Practice', *Gender and Education* 15(1), pp. 91–103

Davis, A.Y. (1981), *Women, Race, and Class*. New York: Random House

Dawkins, C. (2010), 'Beyond Wages and Working Conditions: A Conceptualization of Labor Union Social Responsibility', *Journal of Business Ethics*, 95(1), 129–143

DeMars, W.E. (2005), *NGOs and Transnational Networks: Wild Cards in World Politics*. London: Pluto Press

Diamond, L. (1994), 'Rethinking civil society: toward democratic consolidation', *Journal of Democracy*, 5, pp. 4–18

Dickens L. (1997), 'Gender, race and employment equality in Britain: Inadequate strategies and the role of industrial relations actors', *Industrial Relations Journal* 28(4), pp. 282–289

Dickens, L. (1999), 'Beyond the Business Case: A Three-Pronged Approach to Equality Action', *Human Resource Management Journal*, 9(1), pp. 9–19

Dickens, L. (2007), 'The Road is Long: Thirty Years of Equality Legislation in Britain', *British Journal of Industrial Relations*, 45(3), pp. 463–494

Eade, D. (2004), 'Editorial Overview', *Development in Practice*, 14(1–2), pp. 5–12

Egels-Zanden, N. and Hyllman, P. (2011), 'Differences in Organizing Between Unions and NGOs: Conflict and Cooperation Among Swedish Unions and NGOs', *Journal of Business Ethics*, 101, pp. 249–261

Erel, U., Haritaworn, J., Gutíerrez Rodríguez, E., and Klesse, C. (2008), 'On the depoliticisation of intersectionality talk: conceptualising multiple oppressions in critical sexuality studies', in: Kuntsman, A and Miyake, E (eds), *Out of place: interrogating silences in queerness/raciality*. York: Raw Nerve Book

ETUC (2007), *Women in trade unions: bridging the gap*. Brussels: ETUC

ETUC (2011), *Trade unions and the disability movement: together for a more inclusive labour market*. Brussels: ETUC

ETUC (2011), *ETUC Strategy Action Plan (2011–2015)*. Brussels: ETUC

Eurobarometer (2012), *Eurobarometer 2012 on perceptions of discrimination in the EU*, Special Eurobarometer 393, European Commission

Eurofound (2012a), *NEETs Young people not in employment, education or training: Characteristics, costs and policy responses in Europe*. Luxembourg: Publications Office of the European Union

Eurofound (2012b), *Third European Quality of Life Survey – Quality of life in Europe: Impacts of the crisis*. Luxembourg: Publications Office of the European Union

Eurofound (2013), *Third European Quality of Life Survey – Quality of life in Europe: Social inequalities*. Luxembourg: Publications Office of the European Union

European Commission (2001), *European Governance: a White Paper*. Brussels: European Commission COM

European Commission (2009), 'Economic crisis in Europe: causes, consequences and responses', *European Economy*, 7. Brussels: Directorate-General for Economic and Financial Affairs of the European Commission

European Commission (2009), *The role of NGOs and trade unions in combating discrimination*, European Commission, available at: http://ec.europa.eu/progress

European Commission (2010), *Trade union practices on anti-discrimination and diversity. European Trade Union Anti-Discrimination and Diversity study: Innovative and significant practices in fighting discrimination and promoting diversity.* Luxembourg: Office of the European Union

European Commission (2012), *Discrimination in the EU in 2012*, Special Eurobarometer 393

European Commission (2012), *Report on the application of EU Charter of Fundamental Rights*, Brussels

European Commission (2013), *Council Recommendation on effective Roma integration measures in the Member States.* Brussels: COM

European Trade Union Committee for Education (2006), *Developing non-discriminatory quality education for Roma children 2004–2006.* ETUCE

European Trade Union Institute (ETUI) (2012), *Benchmarking Working Europe 2012.* Brussels: ETUI

European Union Agency for Fundamental Rights (FRA) (2013), 'EU LGBT survey results', available at: http://fra.europa.eu/en/publication/2013/eu-lgbt-survey-european-union-lesbian-gay-bisexual-and-transgender-survey-results (accessed in May 2014)

Ewing, K.D. (2005), 'The Function of Trade Unions', *Industrial Law Journal*, 34(1), pp. 1–22

Fanelli, C., and Brogan, P. (2014), 'Austerity, labour and social mobilizations: rebuilding trade union and working class politics', *Studies in Social Justice*, 8(2), pp. 113–117

Flanders, A. (1970), *Management and Unions.* London: Faber & Faber

Flynn, M., Upchurch, M., Muller-Camen, M., and Schroder, H. (2013), 'Trade union responses to ageing workforces in the UK and Germany', *Human Relations*, 66(1), pp. 45–64

Foden, D. (1999), 'European Employment Policy: Progress without too Narrow Confines', in: E. Gabaglio and R. Hoffmann (eds), *The European Trade Union Yearbook 1998.* Brussels: ETUI

Ford, M. (2006), 'After Nunukan: The Regulation of Indonesian Migration to Malaysia', in: Kaur, A., and Metcalfe, I., *Mobility, Labour Migration and Border Controls in Asia.* New York: Palgrave Macmillan

Foster, D., and Fosh, P. (2009), 'Negotiating 'difference': representing disabled employees in the British workplace', *British Journal of Industrial Relations*, 48(3), pp. 560–582

Foster, D., and Williams, L. (2010), 'The past, present and future of equality agendas: problems of intersectionality in theory and practice', in: Blyton, P., Heery, E., and Turnbull, D. (eds), *Reassessing the Employment Relationship.* Chippenham: Palgrave MacMillan, pp. 318–42

Fraser, N. (1995), 'From Redistribution to Recognition? Dilemmas of Justice in a "Postsocialist" Age', *New Left Review*, I/212

Fredman, S. (2005), 'Double trouble: multiple discrimination and EU law', *European Anti-Discrimination Law Review*, 2, pp. 13–18

Fulton, L. (2013), *Worker representation in Europe*. Labour Research Department and ETUI

Gallin, D. (2000), *Trade Unions and NGOs: A Necessary Partnership for Social Development*, United Nations Research Institute for Social Development (UNRISD)

Gedalof, I. (2013), 'Sameness and difference in government equality talk', *Ethnic and Racial Studies*, 36(1)

Gerards, J. (2007), 'Discrimination Grounds', in: Schiek, D., Waddington, L., and Bell, M. (eds), *Cases, Materials and Text on National, Supranational and International Non-Discrimination Law*. Oxford and Portland: Hart Publishing, pp. 33–184

Giddings, P. (1984), *When and Where I Enter: The Impact of Black Women on Race and Sex in America*. New York: Bantam Books

Gold, M., and Rees, C. (2013), 'What makes an effective European works council? Considerations based on three case studies', *Transfer: European Review of Labour and Research*, 19(4), pp. 539–551

Greene A.M., and Kirton, G. (2004), *Views from another stakeholder: Trade union perspectives on the rhetoric of 'Managing Diversity'*, Warwick papers in Industrial Relations, No 74, Industrial Relations Research Unit University of Warwick

Greve, B. (2009), *The labour market situation of disabled people in European countries and implementation of employment policies: a summary of evidence from country reports and research studies, Report prepared for the Academic Network of European Disability experts* (ANED)

Gumbrell-McCormick, R., and Hyman, R. (2013), *Trade Unions in Western Europe: Hard Times, Hard Choices*. Oxford University Press

Hannet, Sarah (2003), 'Equality at the Intersections: The Legislative and Judicial Failure to Tackle Multiple Discrimination', *Oxford Journal of Legal Studies*, 23(1), p. 68

Harvey, D (2005), *A Brief History of Neoliberalism*. Oxford: Oxford University Press

Healy, G., and Kirton, G. (2000) 'Women, Power, and Trade Union Government', *British Journal of Industrial Relations*, 38(3), pp. 343–360

Healy, G., Kirton, G., and Noon, M. (eds) (2010), *Equality, Inequalities and Diversity*. Basingstoke: Palgrave

Heery, E. (2006), 'Equality Bargaining: Where, Who, Why?', *Gender, Work and Organization*, 13(6)

Heery, E., and Kelly, J. (1988), 'Do female representatives make a difference? Women full-time officials and trade union work', *Work, Employment and Society*, 2(4), pp. 487–505

Heidemann, W. (2002), *Lifelong Learning: Current Developments within Social Dialogue in Selected European Countries*. Düsseldorf: Hans Böckler Stiftung

Herod, A. (2001), 'Labor Internationalism and the Contradictions of Globalization: Or, Why the Local Is Sometimes Still Important in a Global Economy', *Antipode*, 33(3), pp. 407–426

Heyes, J., Lewis, P., and Clark, I. (2012), 'Varieties of capitalism, neoliberalism and the economic crisis of 2008', *Industrial Relations Journal*, 43(3), pp. 222–41

Hodson, R. (2001) *Dignity at Work*. Cambridge: Cambridge University Press

Holgate J., Abbott, S., Kamenou, N., Kinge, J., Parker, J., and Sayce, S. (2012), 'Equality and diversity in employment relations: do we practise what we preach?', in: *Equality, Diversity and Inclusion*, 31(4), pp. 323–339

hooks, b. (1981), *Ain't I a Woman*. Boston: South End Press

hooks, b. (2000), 'Racism and feminism', in: Back, L., and Solomos, J. (eds), *Theories of race and racism: a reader*. London: Routledge

Hopgood, S. (2006), *Keepers of the flame*. Ithaca, NY: Cornell University Press

Hoque, K., and Bacon, N. (2014), 'Unions, joint regulation and workplace equality policy and practice in Britain: evidence from the 2004 Workplace Employment Relations Survey', *Work, Employment & Society* [Published online]

Hudock, A.C. (1999), *NGOs and Civil Society: Democracy by Proxy?*. Cambridge: Polity Press

Hyman, R., Klarsfeld, A., Ng, E., and Hac, R. (2012), 'Introduction: Social regulation of diversity and equality', *European Journal of Industrial Relations*, 18(279), pp. 279–292

International Labour Office (ILO) (2011), *Global Employment Trends 2011*. Geneva: International Labour Office

International Labour Office (ILO) (2007), *Equality at work: Tackling the challenges*. Geneva: ILO Publications

International Labour Office (ILO) (2010), *World of Work Report 2010 From one crisis to the next?*. Geneva: ILO Publications

International Trade Union Confederation (2011), *Never work alone: Trade Unions and NGOs joining forces to combat Forced Labour and Trafficking in Europe*. Brussels: ITUC

Jefferys, S., and Ouali, N. (2007), 'Trade unions and racism in London, Brussels and Paris public transport', *Industrial Relations Journal*, 38, pp. 406–422

Kaler, J. (2001), 'Diversity, equality, morality', in: Noon, M., and Ogbonna, E. (eds), *Equality, diversity and disadvantage in employment*. Basingstoke: Palgrave, pp. 51–64

Kamp, A., and Hagedorn-Rasmussen, P. (2004), 'Diversity management in a Danish context: towards a multicultural or segregated working life', *Economic and industrial democracy*, 25(4), pp. 525–554

Kandola, R., and Fullerton, J. (1998), *Managing the Mosaic: Diversity in Action*, 2nd ed. London: Institute of Personnel Development

Karamessini, M., and Rubery. J. (2013), *Women and Austerity*. Abingdon: Routledge

Karanikolos, M., Mladovsky, P., Cylus, J., Thomson, S., Basu, S., Stuckler, D., Mackenbach, J.P., and McKee, M. (2013), 'Financial crisis, austerity, and health in Europe', *Lancet*, 381(9874), pp. 1323–31

Kenny, M. (2006), *The Politics of Identity*. Cambridge: Polity Press

Kersley, B., Alpin, C., Forth, J., Bryson, A., Bewley, H., Dix, G., and Oxenbridge, S. (2006), *Inside the Workplace: Findings from the 2004 Workplace Employment Relations Survey*. London: Routledge

Kirton, G., and Green, A. (2006), 'The discourse of diversity in unionised contexts: views from trade union equality officers', *Personnel Review*, 35(4), pp. 431–48

Kirton, G., and Greene, A.M. (2010), *The Dynamics of Managing Diversity: A Critical Approach*, 3rd ed. Oxford: Butterworth-Heinemann

Kofman, E., and Sales, R. (1992), 'Towards Fortress Europe?' *Women's Studies International Forum*, 15(1), pp. 129–139

Kosa, A. (2013), *Draft Report on Implementation of Council Directive 2000/78/EC of 27 November 2000 establishing a general framework for equal treatment in employment and occupation (2012/2324)* (INI)

Kretsos, L. (2011), 'Union responses to the rise of precarious youth employment in Greece', *Industrial Relations Journal*, 42(5), pp. 453–472

Krizsan, A., Skeije, H., and Squires, J. (eds) (2012), *Institutionalising Intersectionality: Comparative European Analyses*. Houndmills: Palgrave MacMillan

Lang, S. (2012), *NGOs, Civil Society, and the Public Sphere*. Cambridge: Cambridge University Press

Lansdown, G. (2011), *The right of Roma children to education: position paper*. Geneva: UNICEF Regional Office for Central and Eastern Europe and the Commonwealth of Independent States

Larsson, B. (2012), 'Obstacles to transnational trade union cooperation in Europe – results from a European survey', *Industrial Relations Journal*, 43(2), pp. 152–170

Larsson, B., Bengtsson, M., and Lovén Seldén, K. (2012), 'Transnational trade union cooperation in the Nordic Countries', *Management Revue*, 23(1), pp. 32–48

Lecher, W., Platzer, W.H., Rub, S., and Weiner, P. (2001), *European Works Councils: developments, types and networking*. Aldershot: Gower

Leontidou, L. (2010), 'Urban social movements in "weak" civil societies: The right to the city and cosmopolitan activism in Southern Europe', *Urban Studies*, 47(6)

Leschke J., and Jepsen, M. (2011), 'The economic crisis – challenge or opportunity for gender equality in social policy outcomes? A comparison of Denmark, Germany and the UK', *Working Paper 2011.04*, European Trade Union Institute

Lewis, D. (2010), 'Nongovernmental Organizations, Definition and History', in: Anheier, H.K., and Toepler, S. (eds), *Encyclopaedia of Civil Society*, 1st ed. New York: Springer

Lewis, D. and Kanji, N. (2009), *Non-governmental organizations and development*. London: Routledge

Lewis, T. (2010), *Multiple Discrimination: A Guide to Law and Evidence*. A Central London Law Centre Publication

Litvin, D. (2006), 'Diversity: Making space for a better case', in: Konrad, A., Prasad, P., and Pringle, J. (eds), *Handbook of Workplace Diversity*. Thousand Oaks, CA: Sage

Lorde, A. (1998), 'Age, race, class, and sex: Women redefining difference', in: Anderson, M.L., and Collins, P.H. (eds), *Race, class, and gender: An anthology*. Belmont, CA: Wadsworth, pp. 187–195

Makkonen, T. (2002), *Multiple, compound and intersectional discrimination: bringing the experiences of the most marginalized to the fore*. Institute for Human Rights, Abo Akademi University

Makkonen, T. (2007), *European Handbook on Equality Data*. European Commission, Directorate-General for Employment, Social Affairs and Equal Opportunities, Luxembourg

Marginson, P. (2000), 'The Eurocompany and Euro industrial relations', *European Journal of Industrial Relations*, 6(1), pp. 9–34

Marschall, M. (2002), *Legitimacy and Effectiveness: Civil Society Organizations' Role in Good Governance*, Poverty Reduction Strategies Forum, 29 October–1 November 2002, Baden, Austria

Martin, J., and Roberts, C. (1984), *Women and Employment, a Lifetime Perspective*. London: HMSO

Martinez Lucio, M., and Weston, S. (2000), 'European Works Councils and flexible regulation: the politics of intervention', *European Journal of Industrial Relations*, 6(2), pp. 203–16

McCrudden, C. (2003), 'The New Concept of Equality', *ERA Forum*, 3, pp. 9–29

McKay, S. (2011), 'Does one size fit all? Trade unions, discrimination and legal regulation in the European Union, *The International Journal of Comparative Labour Law and Industrial Relations*, 27(2), pp. 165–188.

McKay, S., Jefferys, S., Paraskevopoulou, A., and Keles, J. (2012), *Study on precarious work and social rights*, European Commission

Mendelson, S.E., and Glenn, J.K. (eds) (2002), *The Power and Limits of NGOs: A Critical Look at Building Democracy in Eastern Europe and Eurasia*. New York: Columbia University Press

Mercer, C. (2002), 'NGOs, civil society and democratization: a critical review of the literature', *Progress in Development Studies*, 2, p. 5

Metcalf, D., Hansen, K., and Charlwood, A. (2001), 'Unions and the sword of justice: unions and pay systems, pay inequality, pay discrimination and low pay', *National Institute Economic Review*, 276(1), pp. 61–75

Mohanty, C.T. (1992), 'Feminist Encounters: Locating the Politic of Experience', in: Barrett, M., and Phillips, A. (eds), *Destabilizing Theory. Contemporary Feminist Debates*. Cambridge: Polity Press, pp. 74–93

Moon, Gay (2006), 'Multiple discrimination – problems compounded or solutions found?', in: *Justice Journal*, 3(2), pp. 86–102

Moore, S., and Wright, T. (2012), 'Shifting models of equality? Union Equality Reps in the public services', *Industrial Relations Journal*, 43(5), pp. 433–447

Moore, S., Wright, T., and Conley, H. (2012), *Addressing discrimination in the workplace on multiple grounds – the experience of trade union Equality Reps*, Research paper, ACAS

Muller, A. (2011), 'Employment Protection Legislation Tested by the Economic Crisis: a global review of the regulation of collective dismissals for economic reasons', *DIALOGUE in Brief No. 3*. Geneva: ILO

Noon, M. (2007), 'The fatal flaws of diversity and the business case for ethnic minorities', in: *Work Employment Society*, 21, p. 773

Noon, M., and Hoque, K. (2001), 'Ethnic minorities and equal treatment: the impact of gender, equal opportunities policies and trade unions', *National Institute Economic Review*, 176(1), pp. 105–127

OECD (2011), *Divided We Stand: Why Inequality Keeps Rising*. OECD Publishing

OECD (2013), *International Migration Outlook 2013*. OECD Publishing

Ozbilgin, M., and Tatli, A. (2011), 'Mapping out the field of equality and diversity: Rise of individualism and voluntarism', *Human Relations*, 64, pp. 1229–1258

Paraskevopoulou, A. (2010), 'The impact of the Racial Equality Directive: a survey of trade unions and employers in the Member States of the European Union, Greece', in: *The impact of the Racial Equality Directive Views of trade unions and employers in the European Union*, Fundamental Rights Agency, available at: http://fra.europa.eu/fraWebsite/attachments/RED_Greece.pdf

Phillips, A. (2004), 'Defending Equality of Outcome', *Journal of Political Philosophy*, 12(1), pp. 1–19

Phoenix, A., and Pattynama, P. (2006), 'Intersectionality', *European Journal of Women's Studies*, 13(3), pp. 187–192

Pulignano, V. (2005), 'EWCs' cross-national employee representative coordination: a case of trade union cooperation?', *Economic and Industrial Democracy*, 26, pp. 383–412

Rifkin, J. (2004), *The European Dream: How Europe's Vision of the Future is Quietly Eclipsing the American Dream*. Cambridge: Polity Press

Rivest, C. (1996), 'Voluntary European Works Councils', *European Journal of Industrial Relations*, 2(2), pp. 235–253

Roman, J. (2004), 'The Trade Union Solution or the NGO Problem? The Fight for Global Labour Rights', *Development in Practice*, 14(1–2), pp. 100–109

Roosevelt, T.R. (1990), 'From Affirmative Action to Affirming Diversity', *Harvard Business Review*, 68(2), pp. 107–117

Roseberry, L. (2011), 'Multiple discrimination', in: Sargeant, M., *Age discrimination and diversity: multiple discrimination from an age perspective*. Cambridge: Cambridge University Press

Rubery, J. (2013), 'Public sector adjustment and the threat to gender equality', in: Vaughan-Whitehead, D. (ed.), *Public sector shock: The impact of policy retrenchment in Europe*. Cheltenham: Edward Elgar

Salamon, L.M. (1994), 'The rise of the non-profit sector', *Foreign Affairs*, 73(4), pp. 109–122

Salamon, L.M., and Anheier, H.K. (1992), 'In Search of the Non-Profit Sector. I: The Question of Definitions', *VOLUNTAS*, 3(2), pp. 125–151

Sargeant, M. (2013), 'Young people and age discrimination', *E-Journal of International and Comparative Labour Studies*, 2(1), pp. 1–16

Sargent, L. (ed.) (1981), *Women and Revolution. The Unhappy Marriage of Marxism and Feminism: A Debate on Class and Patriarchy*. London: Pluto

Schiek, D. (2011), 'Organising EU non-discrimination law around the nodes of "race" gender and disability?', in: Schiek, D., and Lawson, A., (eds), *EU Non-Discrimination Law and Intersectionality: investigating the triangle of racial, gender and disability discrimination*. Farnham: Ashgate

Sen, A.K. (1985), *Commodities and capabilities*. Amsterdam: North Holland

Sen, A.K. (1992), *Inequality re-examined*. Oxford: Clarendon Press

Serrano, M., Xhafa, E., Fichter, M. (eds) (2011), *Trade unions and the global crisis: Labour's visions, strategies and responses*. Geneva: International Labour Office

Sheppard, C. (2011), *Multiple Discrimination in the World of Work*. Geneva: International Labour Organization (ILO)

Simms, M., Eurofound (2011), *Helping young workers during the crisis: contributions by social partners and public authorities*, European Industrial Relations Observatory (EIRO) Comparative analytical report

Spooner, D. (2004), 'Trade unions and NGOs: the need for cooperation', *Development in Practice*, 14(1–2), pp. 19–33

Squires, J. (2008), 'Intersecting Inequalities: Reflecting on the Subjects and Objects of Equality', *The Political Quarterly*, 79(1), January–March 2008

The Economist (2003), 'Who guards the guardians', *The Economist*, conservation, 20 September 2003

Thompson, N. (2011), *Promoting Equality Working with Diversity and Difference*, 3rd ed. Basingstoke: Palgrave McMillan

Tomlinson, F., and Schwabenland, C. (2010), 'Reconciling competing discourses of diversity? The UK non-profit sector between social justice and the business case', *Organization*, 17(1), pp. 101–121

Vaiou, D. (2014), 'Tracing aspects of the Greek crisis in Athens: Putting women in the picture', *European Urban and Regional Studies*, 26 March 2014 (published online before print)

Vakil, A.C. (1997), 'Confronting the classification problem: Toward a taxonomy of NGOs', *World Development*, 25, pp. 2057–2070

Valentine, G., and McDonald, I. (2004), *Understanding prejudice: Attitudes towards minorities*. Stonewall

Van Reenen, J. (2011), 'Wage Inequality, Technology and Trade: 21st Century Evidence', *Labour Economics*, 18(6), pp. 730–41

Verloo, M. (2006), 'Multiple Inequalities, Intersectionality and the European Union', *European Journal of Women's Studies*, 13(3), p. 211

Vertovec, S. (2007), 'Super-diversity and its implications', *Ethnic and Racial Studies*, 29(6), pp. 1024–1054

Villa, P., and Smith, M. (2010), *Gender equality, employment policies and the crisis in EU Member States: Synthesis report 2009*, Expert report commissioned by and presented to the European Commission Directorate-General Employment, Social Affairs and Equal Opportunities

Waddington, J., and Hoffmann, R. (eds) (2000), *Trade unions in Europe: facing challenges and searching for solutions*. Brussels: ETUI

Walby, S. (2013), 'Finance versus democracy? Theorizing finance in society', *Work, Employment and Society*, 27(3), pp. 489–507

Washington, M., and McKay, S. (2011), 'The Controversy over Montréal: The creation of the Outgames in the field of gay and lesbian sports', *Canadian Journal of Administrative Sciences/Revue Canadienne des Sciences de l'Administration*, pp. 467–479

Watson, T.J. (2008), *Sociology, Work and Industry*, 5th ed. London: Routledge

Wilkinson, R., and Pickett, K. (2009), *The spirit level: why more equal societies almost always do better*. London: Penguin

Willetts, P. (2011), *Non-Governmental Organisations in World Politics: The Construction of Global Governance*. Abingdon: Routledge

Wrench, J. (2005), 'Diversity management can be bad for you', *Race and Class*, 46(3), pp. 73–84

Wrench, J., and Virdee, S. (1996), 'Organising the Unorganised: "Race", Poor Work and Trade Unions', in: Ackers, P., Smith, C., and Smith, S. (eds), *The New Work-place and Trade Unionism*. London: Routledge

Yuval-Davis, N. (2006), 'Belonging and the Politics of Belonging', *Patterns of Prejudice*, 40(3), pp. 196–213

Zick, A., Pettigrew, T.F., and Wagner, U. (2008), 'Ethnic prejudice and discrimination in Europe', *Journal of Social Issues*, 64(2), pp. 233–251

Index